CONCILIUM

THEOLOGY IN THE AGE OF RENEWAL

CONCILIUM

CONCILIUM/VOL. 43

PASTORAL THEOLOGY

THE IDENTITY
OF THE PRIEST

edited by KARL RAHNER, S.J.

VOLUME 43

CONCILIUM
theology in the age of renewal

PAULIST PRESS
NEW YORK, N.Y./PARAMUS, N.J.

PAULIST PRESS
EXECUTIVE OFFICES: 304 W. 58th Street, New York, N.Y. and 404 Sette
   Drive, Paramus, N.J.
Publisher: John A. Carr, C.S.P.

EDITORIAL OFFICES: 304 W. 58th Street, New York, N.Y.
Executive Editor: Kevin A. Lynch, C.S.P.
Managing Editor: Urban P. Intondi

Printed and bound in the United States of America by
Wickersham Printing Co., Lancaster, Pa.

CONTENTS

PART II

BIBLIOGRAPHICAL SURVEY

PART III

DOCUMENTATION CONCILIUM
Office of the Executive Secretary
Nijmegen, Netherlands

PREFACE

Karl Rahner, S.J./*Münster, West Germany*
Karl Lehmann/*Mainz, West Germany*
Heinz Schuster/*Saarbrücken, West Germany*

It is hardly necessary to explain why the volume on Pastoral Theology should be wholly devoted to the identity of the priest in the modern world. The various crises besetting the priestly calling can be observed everywhere, and it would be senseless to ignore the problems involved. In planning this volume we have therefore assumed that, insofar as the priestly office and the manner in which a priest understands himself are concerned, we are in a period of transition brought about by theological and social factors. The enduring theological nature of the priestly office in Catholicism leaves enough dogmatic latitude to cope with the priestly ministry in the form required for our phase in the course of the history of the Church.

Accordingly, this volume is written with the consciousness of this critical situation of change and transition, without losing sight of the enduring character of the Church and the priesthood. The first article deals with biblical theology and shows the inner diversity, the various forms and the historically conditioned elements in the way the New Testament sees the ministry and ministers in the Church. Subsequent articles will then point out how the New Testament provides us with various starting points from which we can reach a theological understanding of the priesthood. Unfortunately, and in spite of a great deal of trouble, it

1

has not been possible to find an author to deal with the historical evolution of the "priestly office" in such questions as where in the New Testament we find important points of contact for the "development", what features of historically conditioned mentalities gave rise to eventual changes, what specific cultural and ecclesiastical sociological elements have influenced the shaping of the classical image of the priest, and how the change actually did come about.

Against such a background the present changes would probably not appear to be so "exciting", "destructive" or "arbitrary" if we had a more concrete picture of the intensity, the inevitability and the extent of the changes. A sociological article concerns itself with a theological problem: the way that the "priestly office", in a society marked by distribution of labor, specialization and professionalization, has monopolized various functions and services and gravely affected the classical image of the priest. This helps us to understand that loss of sense of "belonging" and of identity which so many priests experience today. We must take a new look at the traditional structures which frame a priest's life and work: his relationship with the bishop, with other priests, and with the laity, the territorial structure of the parishes and the practical axioms that determine the way in which a priest commits himself in actual reality, the communal or collective forms of life for secular priests (illustrated in this volume with the case of Poland by a bishop of Eastern Europe) and the relations between the diocesan clergy and the regular or secular religious institutes. The reasons behind the contributions regarding the attitude of priests toward revolutionary tendencies and the Bibliographical Survey about the present state of the discussion on celibacy will be explained in their own introductions.

The problems dealt with in this issue in no way exhaust all the important difficulties implied in this general subject. Much of what has been said here (e.g., about the various theological starting points of the priesthood by Kaspar, Hastings, Pin and Rahner) cannot be summarized into a simple synthesis. Again, much that points into a new direction (e.g., in the matter of pastoral care, the concrete expression of spirituality, the external conditions for a "common life", and so on) remains necessarily still somewhat abstract and on the level of principles. However, we have made a start. Both editors and collaborators were determined to get beyond such catchwords as "de-sacralization", "secularization", "de-ideologization" and "de-patriarchalizing".

No one can choose the situation of his own life as he likes it. Today the Church and the priests have the great task and the often apparently intolerable burden to guide us through this transition period in faith and hope. The uncertainties about the priestly image of tomorrow which oppress us today and throw us into frankly admitted confusion can nevertheless coexist with the clear and firm conviction of the belief that there will always be a priestly office in the Church of Jesus Christ.

PART I
ARTICLES

Karl Schelkle/*Tübingen, West Germany*

Ministry and Minister in the New Testament Church

I

THE NOTION OF PRIEST

There were many priests of many gods in both the Jewish and pagan environment of the New Testament.[1] In the wider Greek culture and that of Jewish Hellenism the word for such a priest was *hiereus*. This word is also used in the New Testament for Jewish (Mk. 1, 44; Lk. 1, 5; 10, 31f.; Jn. 1, 9; Acts 6, 7) as well as for pagan priests (Acts 14, 13).

The Priesthood in Jerusalem and at Qumran

At the time of the New Testament there existed in Jerusalem an aristocratic upper class of priests who enjoyed political and social prominence. The lower class of priests was numerous but not greatly respected. The class of scribes dominated that of the priests. In the judgment of the Qumran community, unholy priests discharged an unholy service in Jerusalem (1 QpH 9, 4f.). The high priest of Jerusalem persecuted the Qumran community and its teachers (1 QpH 8, 8-13; 9, 1-12; 12, 6-10). On the other hand, the Qumran community appears to have been founded by priests and to have its own priests (1 Q S 8, 1). They

---

[1] On this point I must mention particularly the following articles from *Theol. Wörterb. z. N.T.*: K. H. Rengstorf, "Apostolos" (I, 1933), pp. 406-46; W. H. Beyer, "Diakonos" (II, 1935), pp. 81-93; *idem*, "Episkopos" (II, 1935), pp. 604-17; G. Schrenk, "Hiereus" (III, 1938), pp. 257-84; G. Bornkamm, "Presbys" (VI, 1959), pp. 651-83.

preached the saving deeds of God (1 Q S 1, 18-21), counseled the community and gave it their blessing (1 Q S 2, 1-4; 6, 3-5). Of the two Messiahs that would appear on the last day one would be a king of the line of David and the other a priest of the line of Aaron (1 Q S 9, 11; 1 Q Sa 2, 11-21). The Qumran community rejected every kind of material sacrifice and only practiced the spiritual sacrifice of prayer and atonement (1 Q S 9, 3-5; CD 6, 12). In the last days the Qumran community will be the true priestly community (1 Q M 2, 5). Some of these Qumran elements point to the way in which the New Testament understood the priesthood.

The Rejection of the Usual Idea of the "Priest" in the New Testament

The New Testament never gives a minister of the Church the current name of *hiereus*—i.e. priest. The reason may lie in the religious sociological situation, since the importance and prestige of the priestly class were at a low ebb at that time in Israel. It is however more probably a matter of religious history, since the content of the word "priest" was fixed by the history and practice of the various religions. It meant the servant of the deity who stood between the deity and the people with the exclusive function of mediating reconciliation or salvation, and who did this particularly through a ritual sacrifice and by acting as a mantic oracle. Since the New Testament rejects this current word for "priest", it is clear that there was no priesthood of this kind in the New Testament community. Only centuries afterward, and not without some hesitation, did the Greek word *hiereus* (which corresponds in Latin to *sacerdos*) make its entry into the Church. On one occasion, Tertullian refers to the bishop as the "high priest" (*summus sacerdos: On Baptism,* 17); Hippolytus, in his *Refutation of All Heresies* 1, 6, also mentions the "high priesthood" (*archieratia*) once and applies it to the apostles. It was not until Eusebius (*History of the Church* 10, 4, 2) that the clergy of the Church were called *hiereis* (priests) in a formal address.

Christ, the True High Priest

The New Testament, however, does use the word "priest" in a very significant way. In the Epistle to the Hebrews (2, 17; 4, 14; 5, 10) Christ is called the true high priest (*archiereus*) who fulfills the Israelite tradition of the high priesthood. Christ offers a priestly sacrifice in obediently fulfilling the will of God (5, 7; 10, 7), in overcoming temptations and suffering (2, 18; 4, 15), and finally in his total surrender at death (7, 27). Just as the principal task of the Old Testament high priest was to reconcile the people at the feast of Atonement, so Christ brought about reconciliation (2, 17), purification (9, 14) and sanctification (9, 13). Since Christ as man shared man's condition (2, 18; 4, 15) as a brother (2, 15), he is a "priest" who understands all, is capable of "feeling with us" (4, 15; 5, 1) and can help (2, 18). As a true priest must be concerned for those in his charge, so Christ, full of compassion, intercedes for the brethren (2, 17; 7, 25). If the Epistle to the Hebrews, probably written about 90 A.D., speaks in such terms of the one high priest Christ, there is no room for another autonomous priesthood in the Church. Through Christ who entered the holy of holies as high priest, the Church offers the only possible sacrifice of praise (13, 15f.). The priestly office can only exist insofar as it represents the one high priesthood of Christ.

"Priestly" Attributes Applied to the Church

Other New Testament texts speak of the priestly dignity of the Church. According to 1 Peter 2, 5. 9, the Church of God is "a people set apart", "a holy and royal priesthood", expressions which echo Exodus 19, 6. In this priestly function the Church must "sing the praises of God" (2, 9) and "offer the spiritual sacrifices made acceptable to God through Jesus Christ" (2, 5). This spiritual cult, however, is not something figurative but a cult celebrated at the very heart of reality, in the divine Spirit. This sacrifice is not something independent but only possible through Jesus Christ. He is the sacrifice acceptable to God (2, 5). Israel hoped that she would be the priestly and royal free People of God in the messianic age (Is. 61, 6; 62, 3). This hope is now fulfilled in the Church. Priestly dignity therefore means the free access to God (Rom. 5, 2; Eph. 2, 18) in the freedom of the Word (2 Cor. 3, 12; Eph. 3, 12; Heb. 4, 16; 10, 19). The kingdom may be hidden as yet but will once become manifest as a royal dominion (Mt. 19, 28; Rom. 5, 17).[2]

In the Apocalypse (1, 6; 5, 10; 20, 6) the faithful are called "priests before God", both collectively and individually. This, too, echoes Exodus 19, 6. But while the priestly dignity is attributed to Israel only as a whole, the Apocalypse goes beyond this and applies it to every one of the faithful.

The authors of 1 Peter and the Apocalypse were not known to each other and show no interdependence. If therefore both independently bear witness to the communal priesthood of the Church, it must reflect a profound and general consciousness of this fact.

II
THE EXERCISE OF THE UNIVERSAL PRIESTHOOD

Preaching the Word

The communal priesthood is given practical expression throughout the life of the community of the New Testament. The whole Church is charged with preaching the Word and performing the cult, and this is put into practice. "When you are all prophesying and an unbeliever or uninitiated person comes in, he will find himself analyzed and judged by *everyone*. . . . He will fall on his face and worship God, declaring that God is among you indeed" (1 Cor. 14, 24). Worship is thus credible only when all witness to the Word. In the Jerusalem community "all proclaim the Word of God boldly" (Acts 4, 31). While Paul is in prison and unable to preach, "most of the brothers have taken

[2] K. H. Schelkle, *Die Petrusbriefe. Der Judasbrief* (Freiburg i. Br., [2] 1964), pp. 57-67.

courage in the Lord from these chains of mine and are getting more and more daring in announcing the message without any fear" (Phil. 1, 12-18). The whole community has been enabled to bear witness in this way by God. "All have learned from God" (1 Thess. 4, 9). "You are all full of good intentions, perfectly well instructed and able to advise each other" (Rom. 15, 14). "But you have not lost the anointing that he [God] gave you, and you do not need anyone to teach you" (1 Jn. 2, 27). The whole Church is charged with the ministry of pastoral care. "And this is what we ask you to do, brothers: warn the idlers, give courage to those who are apprehensive, care for the weak and be patient with everyone" (1 Thess. 5, 14).

The Celebration of the Eucharist

The cult, too, was performed by the whole community. The Lord's supper took its origin from that meal which Jesus celebrated with the Twelve as their last meal together on the eve of his death. That only the Twelve heard the commission "Do this in memory of me" (Lk. 22, 19) is the result of the circumstances during those last days of Jesus' life. Yet, the commission was given to the whole Church. Some abuses led Paul to describe the celebration of the supper in Corinth (1 Cor. 11, 17-34). When the apostle was present, he celebrated the eucharistic meal with the community. But what happened when he was not there? Paul's exhortations were addressed to the whole community and not to some particular officials. No doubt, some individual had to make the outward arrangements. Was this individual a simple leader of prayers or a priest in charge of the cult? Did perhaps the whole community perform together in virtue of their priestly character? This does not mean that today we could go back to such a way of celebrating the eucharist. Development has its validity. If, however, new situations were to force the community occasionally to have a liturgy of the Word without a priest, they should be able to do so and celebrate, remembering their original call to the universal priesthood. Paul gave the whole Church the mandate and dignity "to offer God a living, holy and acceptable sacrifice in spiritual worship" through her very being (Rom. 12, 1). "Through Christ let us offer God an unending sacrifice of praise, a verbal sacrifice that is offered every time we acknowledge his name. Keep doing good works and sharing your resources, for these are sacrifices that please God" (Heb. 13, 15).[3]

Church Order

In the Church of the New Testament the "laity" also played their part in Church order, as in preaching and liturgy. A chapter in St. Matthew which has been rightly described as the "oldest Church order" says: "If your brother does something wrong, go and have it out with him alone, between your two selves. If he listens to you, you have won back your brother. If he does not listen, take one or two others along with you: the evidence of two or three witnesses is required to sustain any charge. But if he refuses to listen to these, report it to the community; and if he refuses to listen to the community, treat him like a pagan or a tax collector" (Mt. 18, 15). Justice must be found and done in the face of the Church, not in some secret procedure of authorities. When Paul was forced once, during one of his missionary absences from Corinth, to make an important decision regarding that community, he did not want to do it on the basis of some plenipotentiary quality of his own, but together with the community. This community should meet, and since Paul could not be present in the body, he at least wanted to be there in spirit: the decision was to be made "when you are assembled together in the name of the Lord Jesus, and I am spiritually present with you" (1 Cor. 5, 4).

The Importance of the Laity
at the Beginning of the Church

The New Testament—evidently not intending to give a complete list—names a number of men and women who assisted

[3] J. Beck, "Sakrale Existenz. Das gemeinsame Priestertum des Gottesvolkes als kultische und ausserkultische Wirklichkeit," in *Münchener Theol. Zeitschr.* 19 (1968), pp. 17-34.

the apostles. Sometimes it is said that they were given their function with prayer and an imposition of hands, as in Acts 6, 6; 13, 3; 1 Tim. 4, 4; 5, 22; 2 Tim. 1, 6—texts which it must be admitted are rather late. Therefore, these were ordained. But this hardly applies to all or even to most of them. They were thus mainly "lay" people according to present Canon Law. In the regions surrounding the communities which Paul founded in the large cities, new communities sprang up, like those of Kolossae, Laodicaea and Pergamon in the region around Ephesus. The missionaries who founded these communities were clearly lay people. Themselves well instructed, they were, first of all, messengers and teachers of the Gospel, then the leaders and pastors of the new communities to whom they devoted their energy and ability. The communities met in their houses (Rom. 16, 5. 23; 1 Cor. 16, 19; Col. 4, 5; Acts 2, 4-6; 12, 12; 20, 20). The hospitable and receptive home was the center and nucleus of a community (as already was true in Mt. 10, 12f.; Lk. 10, 5f.; Acts 20, 20). The importance of the "house" communities bears witness to the importance of the laity for the Church at the beginning.

The Part Played by Women
in the Service of the Church

In the New Testament Church, women also shared in the service and functions of the Church. Sometimes people quote Paul's words (1 Cor. 14, 34f.): "Women are to remain quiet at meetings, since they have no permission to speak. . . . If they have any questions to ask, they should ask their husbands at home." But the same apostle says in the same epistle a little before the passage quoted: "For a woman, however, it is a sign of disrespect . . . if she prays or prophesies unveiled" (1 Cor. 11, 5). Both these statements have equal value. A woman was thus entitled to pray publicly in church and to teach as a prophetess. Paul simply asks that she conform to custom and wear a veil. What Paul said in 1 Corinthians 14, 34f. must therefore be understood in the sense that Paul finds it unseemly for women to take part in disputes about points of teaching in the Church. Many scholars, however, find these two statements frankly contradictory. According to them the statement forbidding a woman to speak in the church is not Paul's but a later insertion put in at a time when women's rights were restricted, as we see in 1 Timothy 2, 12: "I am not giving permission for a woman to teach or to tell a man what to do. A woman ought not to speak." Is there no justification for eliminating 1 Corinthians 14, 34 from the original text, since some manuscripts place it after verse 40?

In his epistles Paul mentions many women by name and bestows great praise on them for the service they render to the community. He exhorts the communities to be grateful for this assistance rendered by women. Both Acts (18, 26) and the Pauline epistles (1 Cor. 16, 19; Rom. 16, 3f.) mention the Jewish-Christian couple Aquila and Prisca. Paul says of them: "My greetings to Prisca and Aquila, my fellow workers in Christ Jesus, who risked death to save my life: I am not the only one to owe them a debt of gratitude; all the churches among the pagans do as well." In Romans 16, 2 he mentions a deaconess Phoebe who "rendered many services" to the Church in Cenchreae near Corinth. In Philippians 4, 2 Paul mentions Evodia and Syntyche together with Clement, who "fought for the Gospel" with him. At the end of his Epistle to the Romans, Paul sends greetings to many Christians in Rome by name, and among them a number of women whose work for the Church he praises (Rom. 16, 6. 12ff.).[4]

III
SPECIFIC SERVICES AND FUNCTIONS

Although the New Testament stresses the importance of the Church's body as a whole, it also mentions specific services and functions and those who administered them. Thus it mentions

[4] E. Kähler, *Die Frau in den paulinischen Briefen* (Zurich, 1960); G. Fitzer, *Das Weib schweige in der Gemeinde* (Munich, 1963); G. G. Blum, "Das Amt der Frau im N.T.," in *Novum Testamentum* 7 (1964), pp. 142-62; E. Gössman, "Women as Priests?" in *Concilium* 34 (1968), pp. 115-25.

(Rom. 12, 7; 1 Cor. 12, 8f. 28; Eph. 2, 20; 4, 11; 1 Pet. 2, 25; Acts 20, 28): apostles (in the wider sense, outside the Twelve), pastors, presidents, prophets, evangelists and teachers. The designations of *presbuteros* (Acts 11, 30; 14, 23; 1 Tim. 5, 17), *episkopos* and *diakonos* (Acts 20, 28; Phil. 1, 1; 1 Tim. 3, 2. 8) became particularly important, since these names became part of the Christian language and were incorporated in Canon Law.

Presbyters, Bishops and Deacons

In the Israel of the Old Testament, as in the Judaism of the New, the *presbuteros* ("elder") played an important and basic part both in the local community and in that of the people as a whole. It is difficult to distinguish between the implications of the words "elder" and "official". The Qumran community distinguished between elder and priest (1 Q S 6, 8-10). The titles *episkopos* (bishop), which originally simply meant "overseer", and *diakonos* (deacon), originally simply a servant, are wholly secular. Since both titles occur first in the (Gentile Christian) community of Philippi (Phil. 1, 1), it is possible that they came from the Hellenistic guild system.[5] Bishops and presbyters are sometimes (at first) identical (Acts 20, 17. 28), sometimes (later) distinct (Tit. 1, 5). Herein lies the beginning of a "monarchical" episcopacy.

The Meaning of "Diakonia"

Diakonia is the all-embracing and essential term for "office" in the New Testament. This "office" covers administration (1 Cor. 4, 1f.; Col. 1, 25), the right to lead and to preside (Heb. 13, 17; 1 Thess. 5, 12; Rom. 12, 8), and the competence to judge (Mt. 19, 28) and to punish (1 Cor. 5, 5). But in all this it remains service. Speaking about the disciple's duty toward all, Christ says: "Anyone who wants to be first among you must be a slave to all" (Mk. 10, 44). The parable of the conscientious servant describes the service which binds the disciple (Mt. 24, 45-51; in the parallel passage, Lk. 12, 41-46, the image of the servant is

[5] J. Gnilka, *Der Philipperbrief* (Freiburg i. Br., 1968), pp. 32-40.

applied to the apostles). Paul calls himself the servant of God, of Christ and of the Church (1 Cor. 9, 19; 2 Cor. 4, 5). The apostolic function is simply "service" (Rom. 11, 13; 1 Cor. 3, 5; 2 Cor. 6, 3; Acts 20, 24; 21, 19). The various tasks are no more than an unfolding of the one service, "There are all sorts of service to be done but there is but one Lord" (1 Cor. 12, 5). The building up of the body of Christ is *one* service (Eph. 4, 11). The New Testament uses the words that were currently used in Greek for official functions (such as *arche, time, telos*) only to designate Jewish or secular functions, never ecclesiastical ones. "Order" and justice (or law) in the Church mean something so totally different from order and justice in the world that it is impossible to use the same words for the two.

Various "Services" and "Offices"

Services in the Church are for a large part understood as charisms, as gifts of the Spirit (Rom. 12, 6-8; 1 Cor. 12, 7-11), as direct interventions by God (1 Cor. 11, 28-31) and as gifts of Christ to his Church (Eph. 4, 11f.). Other functions, such as that of the presbyter, probably had from the beginning a juridical connotation (Acts 11, 30; 14, 23, etc.). The various attitudes toward these were evened out. The charism was institutionalized in sacrament and office (1 Tim. 4, 14; 2 Tim. 1, 6). A service became an office when the bearer was commissioned permanently and finally through juridical procedures. The origin of this process can already be found in the call of the apostles. As "fishers of men" those that are called stand permanently between the world and the coming kingdom of God, between past and future, between men and God (Mk. 1, 16-20). They are "created" and sent out as "the Twelve", in order to preach and to "bring in" the whole world (Mk. 3, 14f.; Mt. 10, 1). Their decisions are valid in the kingdom of God. Their activity is God's activity in the present (Mt. 16, 19; 18, 18). Paul says the same thing. Through the apostle's preaching the Word of God is operative in the community (1 Thess. 2, 13). The Church is charged with the Word and the function of reconciliation (2

Cor. 5, 18-20). Her liturgical service makes the people acceptable to God as an offering (Rom. 15, 15-19). The apostles are
the collaborators of God (1 Cor. 3, 9; 1 Thess. 3, 2).

The Function of the "Twelve"

The gospels ascribe the call and commission of the Twelve to
the historical Jesus. The risen Lord sends them finally on their
mission (Mt. 28, 19). One cannot really see the group of Twelve
as a post-resurrection event. The name "apostle", it is true, is of
later date, as the gospels themselves make clear (Mark 3, 14 and
Matthew 10, 2 are earlier than Luke 6, 13). The term *apostolos*
was perhaps chosen by the community in connection with the
verb *apostellein* because it was rarely used in profane language
and could therefore be given a new content.[6]

The original and personal function of the Twelve who were
directly called and sent out by the Lord cannot be repeated or
transmitted. But the task of the apostolic function developed.
The apostles appointed presidents for the communities in their
place (Phil. 1, 1; 1 Tim. 4, 14; 5, 22; 2 Tim. 1, 6; Acts 14, 23).
They must transmit their function to others in turn (1 Tim. 1, 3;
4, 11; Tit. 1, 5; 2 Tim. 2, 1f.). As the Spirit acts through the
Church, they must feed the flock "of which the Holy Spirit has
made you the overseers" (Acts 20, 28). As permanent officials
they stand out in the community as *presbyters,* priests, and stand
over against this community (1 Tim. 5, 17). They already
obtain their living from the community, something which may
become a temptation for them (1 Cor. 9, 14; 1 Pet. 5, 2f.). The
priest is particularly charged with looking after the sick (Jas.
5, 14). Since the healing of the sick is, according to the Gospel, a
sign of the eschatological fulfillment of salvation (Mt. 12, 28;
Lk. 13, 10-17) and since Jesus empowered the apostles to do it

---

[6] B. Rigaux, "The Twelve Apostles," in *Concilium* 34 (1968), pp. 5-15;
D. Müller, "Apostel," in *Bibeltheologisches Wörterbuch* 1 (1968), pp. 31-
38; E. M. Kredel, "Der Apostelbegriff in der neuesten Exegese," in
Zeitschr. f. Kath. Theol. 78 (1956), pp. 257-305; G. Klein, *Der Ursprung
des Zwölfapostolats* (Göttingen, 1961); W. Schmithals, *Das kirchliche
Apostelamt* (Göttingen, 1961); M. Hengel, *Nachfolge und Charisma*
(Berlin, 1968).

(Mt. 10, 8), this expresses something with which the New Testament was concerned from a very early date.[7]

IV
LATER DEVELOPMENTS

The Age of the Fathers

The New Testament taught and practiced the universal priesthood of the Church. The Fathers knew about and spoke of this priestly dignity of the whole Church. Although in their teaching and activity they built up the ecclesiastical hierarchy, they nevertheless stressed the unity of the Church in the class distinction of priests and laity. In a letter (66, 8; cf. 33, 1), St. Cyprian, bishop of Carthage, wrote: "The bishop is in the Church and the Church in the bishop." The bishop is not the Church but represents it, just as the people are represented in the bishop. In his *City of God* (20, 10) St. Augustine says: "We call all Christians priests because they are members of the one priest Christ, just as we call them all anointed because of the mysterious unction; hence the apostle Peter addresses them as 'a holy people and royal priesthood'." In his commentary on the gospel of St. John (124, 7) he explains the Petrine text of Matthew 16, 18 ("I will give you the keys of the kingdom of heaven: whatever you bind on earth shall be considered bound in heaven") as follows: "It is not Peter alone who looses, but the whole Church binds and looses the bonds of sin." "You, too, bind; you, too, loose. For whosoever is bound is separated from your com-

[7] W. Michaelis, *Das Ältestenamt der christlichen Gemeinde im Licht der Heiligen Schrift* (Bern, 1953); H. v. Campenhausen, *Kirchliches Amt und geistliche Vollmacht* (Tübingen, 2 1963); *idem, Die Anfänge des Preisterbegriffes in der alten Kirche: Tradition und Leben* (Tübingen, 1960), pp. 272-89; K. H. Schelkle, *Jüngerschaft und Apostelamt* (Freiburg i. Br., 3 1965); C. Romaniuk, *Le sacerdoce dans le Nouveau Testament* (Le Puy, 1968); E. Käseman, *Amt und Gemeinde im Neuen Testament. Exegetische Versuche und Besinnungen* 1 (Göttingen, 1960), pp. 109-34; W. Marxsen, *Die Nachfolge der Apostel. Der Exeget als Theologe* (Gütersloh, 1968), pp. 75-90.

munity, and whosoever is separated from your community is bound by you; and when the sinner is reconciled, he is loosed by you because you, too, pray to God for him" (*S. Augustini Sermones post Maurinos reperti*, ed. G. Morin, 1930, 16, 2).

The whole Church, endowed with love by the Holy Spirit, forgives sins. St. John Chrysostom, bishop of Constantinople, says in his explanation of the liturgy of the eucharist (*Hom. on II Cor.* 18, 3; PG 61, col. 527): "The eucharist is common to all. It is not only celebrated by the priest but by the people together with him. For he begins only after the faithful have given him their consent by proclaiming: 'It is right and fitting. . . .' " The Fathers were therefore convinced that the whole Church mediates grace, remits sin, sanctifies and conveys life in truth. Throughout antiquity and the Middle Ages there is evidence that the sacraments were not only dispensed by the ecclesiastical official but involved the intersession of the whole Church in the sacramental action.

Under the Spell of Reformation and Counter-Reformation

If the awareness of this communal aspect diminished and almost vanished, it is, like so many other things, the unwanted and unfortunate result of the Reformation and the Counter-Reformation. The Reformation, at the time dominated by Martin Luther, detached the status of the Christian from the bonds which tied it traditionally to the authorities in the Church and did away with ecclesiastical class-distinctions. Every human person, man or woman, was a priest through his baptism and competent to discharge the priestly function. Luther attacked the special priesthood and only recognized the universal priesthood of the whole Church.

And so the official authorities in the old Church and their theologians saw themselves forced to concentrate so heavily on the defense of the then traditional doctrine of the special priesthood that Catholic teaching and practice became frankly one-sided. The biblical and then traditional Catholic doctrine of the universal priesthood remained valid in principle but was pushed into the background by the strong emphasis on the special priesthood; it became obscure and practically forgotten. From many other points of view, too, the doctrine which was common to the Reformation and Counter-Reformation suffered from the exaggerated emphasis on the contrasts between the two. Today we realize that we have to think again about the basic doctrine and rediscover the balanced view.

The Part Played by Vatican Council II

The most recent development in the teaching and life of the Church has led back to a self-awareness of the Church as she existed in the beginning. Vatical Council II quotes 1 Peter 2, 4-10 in its *Decree on the Apostolate of the Laity* (nn. 1-3) and declares that the laity, too, share in the priestly, prophetic and royal function of Christ and play their part in the mission of the People of God in both Church and world. As in Pius XII's encyclical *Mediator Dei,* Vatican Council II described the liturgical function of the universal priesthood. In its *Constitution on the Sacred Liturgy* (n. 48) we read, "By offering the immaculate victim not only through the hands of the priest, but also with him, they should learn to offer themselves."

This change is now becoming visible in Church architecture which has taken the altar away from the back of the choir and placed it near the community so that the priest, turned to the people, represents with this people one celebrating community. The divine service is certainly not only the function of the celebrant but the function of the whole community. Together they celebrate the one service, which is their "service" *tout court.*

We know that for a long time the rubrics prescribed that the priest must pronounce all the prayers in a low voice, even when these prayers were already intoned by servers or the people (e.g., Gloria, Credo, Epistle, Gospel). This could only mean that only what the priest does was thought to be done by the Church and that the hierarchy claimed everything. This has now been done away with; the priest no longer has to mumble what the people have already said aloud. What is performed by the people is performed by the Church.

Walter Kasper/*Münster, West Germany*

A New Dogmatic Outlook on the Priestly Ministry

I

THE PRESENT STATE OF UNCERTAINTY

A proper understanding of the priestly office is one of the critical questions for the post-conciliar Church. The widespread uncertainty surrounding this question and its answer is more and more taking on the character of an acute crisis. The drop in priestly vocations, the debates about the obligation of priestly celibacy, the desire for reforms in the process of priestly formation, the human and vocational crises in the lives of many priests, and the varied antagonisms between the priest and the layman or the priest and his superiors are, to a large extent, merely external symptoms of this worldwide crisis.

The roots of this challenge to the hitherto prevailing understanding of the priestly office are many and varied. Only a few of them can be alluded to in this article. First of all, there is the widespread sociological upheaval and the general tendency toward democratization in our present society. In the past, the ecclesiastical office adopted many of the sociological forms that were current at the time. Thus the Church, in her concrete structures, still maintains many feudal authoritarian elements that are rapidly fading away in society as a whole. This has created inner conflict for many priests, young priests in particular, confronting them with the difficult task of separating the essential, indispensable elements of the former notion of ecclesiastical office

20

from the older forms and working them up into a new, contemporary outlook.

This task is rendered more difficult by a second set of problems that are more strictly theological in nature. The biblical foundation for the priestly office is becoming more and more difficult and elusive. In the history of the Church and Church dogma, the understanding and the exercise of the priestly office have undergone enormous changes. The heavy stress on the responsibility of all Christians makes it more and more difficult to make a clear distinction between the functions of the priestly office and those of the community—i.e., between the various stages of the priestly office. It is obvious that here a wide range of variation is possible.

Finally, we must mention the overall process of secularization in our present society. It has raised considerable problems about the faith for all Christians. The problem is heightened for priests, however, because both their human and their vocational life is based on the faith. Moreover, the traditional image of the priest was greatly conditioned by a notion of the sacred which is no longer practicable in today's secularized world. The priest, in the past, was the person of special holiness, dedicated to cultic worship; in many external matters (dress, style of life, celibacy), he was clearly distinguished from the laity. Now, to the extent that the Church proposes to be present in the world again even in the person of her official representatives, and to the extent that she wishes to avoid retreat into the ghetto of the sacred, she must set aside her older conceptions as hindrances. On the other hand, dogma does suggest that the priestly office is essentially grounded in cultic and sacral functions. Thus we are faced with weighty conflicts and tensions in our attempt to broach a proper understanding of the priestly office.

All these difficulties have raised considerable uncertainty in the minds of many priests about their proper role. To provide a satisfactory solution, we must tackle these problems by the roots and attempt to formulate a new dogmatic understanding of the priestly office. Only by examining fundamentals here can we arrive at correctly structured forms. To be sure, we do not presently possess a solution that will satisfactorily handle all the existing problems; nor will such a solution be found in this article. Our aim here is simpler. Starting out from the New Testament, we propose to suggest a few possible lines of thought that may contribute to a new dogmatic outlook while allowing for the integration and preservation of the essential traditional elements.

II
FOUNDATIONS FOR A NEW OUTLOOK

Christological Foundations

Any theology of the priesthood must start out with the clear and unequivocal teaching of Scripture: there is only one mediator between God and man (1 Tim. 2, 5) and only one high priest—Jesus Christ (Heb. 8, 6; 9, 15; 12, 24). But Jesus Christ is a priest in a way that goes far beyond any other parallels in the history of religions. His contrast to the priesthood of his time is enormous. He breaks through the cultic barriers and directs his attention to the ritually impure, the godless, and the lowest classes of society.

In so doing, he calls into question the distinction between the sacred and the profane that prevaled in antiquity. He enters into all the dimensions of humanity, becoming like us in all things save sin (Heb. 4, 15). In his humanity, he is the visible sign and the concrete embodiment of God's saving love for all men. His human surrender to the Father's will and his service to men are the visible manifestations of God's love.

In Scripture, Christ's priestly work is depicted as abandonment to the Father (Heb. 7, 27; 10, 5ff.) and "for the many" (Mk. 10, 45; 14, 24). The old notion of cultic worship and sacrifice is shattered. Christ's sacrifice does not take place within the precise precincts of a sacred or ritual locale (Heb. 13, 13), but in the visible environment of everyday life in the world. The important thing now is to serve God in love (Rom. 12, 1; 1 Cor. 6, 20)—i.e., in the daily turmoil of worldly existence.

In like manner, Christ also shatters all human notions of

power and lordship. He comes among his disciples as a servant (Lk. 22, 27); true greatness is to be found in rendering service to others (Mk. 9, 35). All man's notions about power and greatness are exploded and turned upside down. They are not to play a role in the thinking of Jesus' disciples; he who would be first must become the servant of all (Mk. 10, 43f.).

The priesthood of Christ, which becomes operative in obedience and service, exists and perdures once for all time (Heb. 9, 12. 26; 10, 10; 1 Pet. 3, 18). Christ is high priest forever (Heb. 6, 20; 7, 3. 24; 10, 14); he intercedes forever with the Father on our behalf (Heb. 7, 25). Through him and in his person, God and the world are definitively reconciled. The priesthood of Christ, then, has no need to be continued or completed by other human priests. It is the consummation of all priesthoods, bringing them to their definitive end. Jesus Christ is the one and only priest of the new covenant. He is the one who baptizes, consecrates and preaches; he is the one who leads the Church.[1]

Now although Christ's priestly work of reconciliation has taken place once for all time, it involves the perduring "ministry of reconciliation". The apostolic ministry, which continues the summons of reconciliation in Christ's name and on his orders, is a constitutive element in Christ's salvific work (2 Cor. 5, 18-20). But it can only be the historical embodiment and organ of Christ's one and only priesthood.

This appreciation of Christ's unique priesthood represents, in purely human terms, the removal of much pressure and responsibility. It frees man from obsessive worries about his weighty responsibility. Because Jesus Christ is the one and only priest, man's responsibility for the salvation of other men becomes bearable and feasible. It is now bearable insofar as we truly believe that Jesus is the Lord, and that history and the future are his. Thus faith in Jesus Christ as the Lord becomes a decisive presupposition for anyone entering the priestly office. Participation in Christ's priesthood is concretized through the obedience of faith and the willingness to serve.

[1] Augustine, *In Ioannem*, tr. 6, Ch. 1, n. 7: PL 35, 1428; Pius XII, *Mystici corporis* (1943), nn. 53, 57; *Constitution on the Sacred Liturgy*, n. 7.

Ecclesiological Foundations

Participation in the priestly ministry of Jesus Christ is primarily an attribute of the Church as a whole (i.e., of his community). Already in the Old Testament, the whole People of God was designated as a priestly people (Ex. 19, 6; Is. 61, 1; 2 Mach. 2, 17). In the New Testament, too, all Christians together are the kingly and priestly people; this people is summoned to proclaim the wondrous works of God and to offer spiritual sacrifice (1 Pet. 2, 5. 9; Apoc. 1, 6; 5, 10). The whole People of God, then, is summoned to witness, to sacrifice, and to kingly leadership.

The priesthood of all Christians is not simply a participation in the official priesthood. Rather, the whole Church as such is the real and primary holder of Christ's salvific mission, and each individual—be he pope, bishop, priest or layman—can only operate in community with the whole Church and as an organ of this whole.[2] It is the Church as a whole, not just the episcopate, that is collegial. To be sure, this collegiality is not to be equated with democracy in the strict sense, since its power comes from Christ rather than from the people (DS 1769, 1777). But many democratic structures could find an analogous application in the Church. The brotherhood and equality of all the members takes precedence over all later distinctions and persists in them.

Now the responsibility and fundamental equality of all does not mean that everyone in the Church can do everything. There are a "variety of ministries" (1 Cor. 12, 5) in the Church, and fundamental differences do exist between them. Paul enumerates the following list of ministries: apostles, prophets, teachers, miracles, gifts of healing, services of help, power of administration, and the speaking of various tongues (1 Cor. 12, 28). This list is hardly exhaustive (cf. Rom. 12, 6ff.; Eph. 4, 11ff.). Depending on the freedom of the Spirit, these charisms can change with changing historical circumstances. But since the Church is built up on the apostles and prophets (Eph. 2, 20), it is not only an apostolic Church but also a Church of charismatic prophecy.

---

[2] *Dogmatic Constitution on the Church*, nn. 10-12, 33ff.

The charisms, then, belong to the perduring structure of the Church.[3]

For Paul, charisms are nothing else but ministries of service within the Church community (Rom. 12, 4; 1 Cor. 12, 4). Every Christian possesses his own charism (1 Cor. 7, 7), and every charism is meant to serve the common good (1 Cor. 12, 7). The charisms are to complement each other and to fit into an integrated whole and the content and test of every charism is love (1 Cor. 13). No one person can possess all the charisms or do everything in the Church; each person must listen to others, for he needs them to correct and fill up his own shortcomings.

This also holds true for the charism of administrative leadership (1 Cor. 12, 8)—that is, for the ecclesiastical magisterium. It cannot take all the other charisms into its hands. Its function is the integration and coordination of all the charisms, not the expropriation of them. It is responsible for the orderly integration and implementation of all the charisms; thus, in a special way, it serves the unity of the Church.[4] In this respect, it is a particularly essential and distinct ministry, but it is a ministry designed to abet and correlate the other ministries of services.

To formulate a new understanding of the priestly office, then, we must begin with the charism of community leadership. This starting point corresponds well with the terminology of Scripture, for Scripture avoids all the prevalent terms for official authority (archē, timē, telos) when it speaks of Church authority. It replaces these terms with words that refer simply to the functions of service and management (diakonia, oikonomia). Scripture also avoids all titles associated with cultic ritual (hereus, sacerdos, pontifex), and it replaces them with titles associated with the secular sphere.

Many of these individual titles are still quite fluid. Paul talks about the charisms of administrative power and leadership (1 Cor. 12, 28), of those who are "over" others (1 Thess. 5, 12;

[3] Ibid., n. 12. On the charismatic structure of the Church, see H. Küng, "The Charismatic Structures of the Church," in Concilium 4 (1965), pp. 41-61; H. Schürmann, "Die geistlichen Gnadengaben," in De Ecclesia I, ed. G. Barauna (Freiburg im Br., 1966), pp. 494-519.

[4] Dogmatic Constitution on the Church, n. 30.

Rom. 12, 8), and of those who "labor among you" (1 Thess. 5, 12; 1 Cor. 16, 16). In the community at Philippi (Phil. 1, 1), we encounter for the first time bishops (*episkopi*) and deacons (*diakoni*). These titles, which were to become so basic later on, were not cultic or sacral at the start. An *episkopos* could be anyone functioning as an overseer of some sort—e.g., governor, policeman, community official, etc. A *diakonos* could be involved in a wide variety of services, from serving table to assisting at official cultic worship.

In the Judaeo-Christian communities, we encounter the *presbyter* (Acts 11, 30; 14, 23; 15, 2; Jas. 5, 14) instead of the *episkopos* and the *diakonos*. Here we are dealing with the notion of the community "elders", which was taken over from the Jewish synagogue; it is the derivation of our own word "priest". In all these titles, the function of community leadership stands in the foreground. It is not viewed in aristocratic terms, however, but in terms of service. It can only be exercised collegially, with the cooperation of all Christians.

The ministerial character of the priestly office is also made clear in the fact that it does not involve a rigid system of officialdom. In Scripture, the office of community leadership varies with varying and changing situations. Different types of communal structures can exist side by side, or follow one another in time. The offices of *episkopos, presbyter* and *diakonos* corresponded to different types of communities. They were originally independent from one another. Only gradually did they develop into the threefold hierarchical arrangement that we are familiar with today; we move from suggestive hints in Acts (20, 17. 28) and the pastoral epistles (Tit. 1, 5. 7) to full development in the epistles of Ignatius of Antioch (Magn. 6, 1; 13, 1; Trall. 3, 1; 7, 2).

Even after the time of Ignatius of Antioch, these designations underwent many changes in the course of Church history and theology.[5] The precise boundary between authoritative office and community, and between the offices themselves, was deter-

[5] J. Guyot (ed.), *Das apostolische Amt* (Mainz, 1961); Y. Congar (ed.), *L'Episcopat et l'Eglise universelle* (Paris, 1962); J. Colson, *L'Episcopat catholique* (Paris, 1963); H. Küng, *Die Kirche* (Freiburg-Basel-Vienna, 1967), pp. 458-522.

mined by the exigencies of the whole sacramental economy; in short, it was determined by the needs of the faithful whom this office was meant to serve. This means that today we have a relatively large amount of freedom in reshaping our understanding and our practical implementation of the priestly office.

Our starting point for determining the essential nature of the ecclesiastical ministry, then, is the charism of leadership—that is, the ministry which serves the unity of the Church. This means that we are not going to describe the priestly office primarily in terms of its sacral-sacramental-consecratory function, but in terms of its socio-ecclesial function. But our starting point must be capable of preserving the essential traditional elements and integrating them into a reasonable whole.

III
OUTLINES OF A NEW DOGMATIC OUTLOOK

Charism and Office

In "de-sacralizing" and "de-mythologizing" the priestly office, we not only do justice to the testimony of Scripture, but we also make the priestly office something that is humanly feasible once again. If we reduce the specific nature of this office to the power to pronounce certain words of consecration, then the priestly office is hardly a human vocation that can satisfy the heart of a young man. If, on the other hand, it involves the task of leading the ecclesial community, then it does indeed involve real human charisms: the ability to meet people and talk with them, the ability to organize and direct human beings, and the capacity for management (in the best sense of that word). Such a task calls for a courteous, responsible and balanced human being, and it demands initiative, imagination and real knowledge of human nature.

This functional presentation of the priestly office should not be misinterpreted as a purely situational reality, for, in the last analysis, it is ontological. In the realm of creatures, interpersonal relations are the highest ontological reality. They determine not only what a man does, but also what he is as a human being. The function of community leadership, then, lays claim on the whole humanity of the priest; it affects him not only in the concrete actions that he performs, but also in what he is as a human being involved in history and human society.

The priestly ministry, then, is never simply a job or one's "life work". Here faith in Jesus becomes something more than the general foundation for one's life as a human being; it becomes the distinctive foundation of one's whole professional existence. Bearing witness to Christ in his professional life, the priest serves as a symbol and a deputy of the community that is entrusted to his care. In both what he is and what he does, he is "for others". In short, the function of community leadership has a thorough-going ontological aspect.

The unity of the Church, which the priestly function is meant to serve, is not just a sociological reality; it is also, and primarily, a theological reality. It is a unity in one Lord and one Spirit; hence it can only be served in and through the Holy Spirit. The ministry of community leadership involves a real theological charism as well as a human charism. The priestly office cannot be carried out by purely sociological functions. On the other hand, we cannot view this charism as something basically inimical to institutional and official structures. There can be no essential split between charism and office.

There is, however, a perduring tension between office and charism, and it is rooted in the interim nature of the Church. Because the Church is "on the road" from the old to the new era, the unity of office and charism is not something "given"; it persists as a duty to be accomplished, and the difference between the two realities is a fact that is experienced by every priest.

This tension between office and charism, which is fundamental to the priestly office, is something that the traditional teaching on the sacrament of orders tried to bring out. On the one hand, the ecclesiastical office does involve a public, visible summons to a public function in the Church—a summons that is issued by the laying on of hands (Acts 6, 6; 14, 23; 1 Tim. 4, 14; 5, 22). But since this function can be performed properly only in faith and ministerial service, it also has need of charisms. Thus the visible, external summons to the ecclesiastical office becomes a promissory and efficacious sign of grace, the grace which is given to the priestly office for the sanctification of others rather than for the priest's personal sanctification (DS 1766; 1773).

The doctrinal teaching on the sacrament of orders also maintains the perduring difference between office and charism, by distinguishing between the "indelible character" of the sacrament and the specific grace of the priestly office.[6] However confusing and open to misinterpretation this teaching may seem to be at first glance, we must not overlook the solid core it contains. The ambiguous term "indelible character", if understood properly, does not refer to some essentially mysterious ontological quality or some metaphysical clerical privilege; it bears witness to the fact that the man called to the priestly office is summoned to serve others with every ounce of humanity that he possesses. His public function in the Church colors everything that he is as a man. And in performing this function, he experiences the difference between what he personally accomplishes and what he is commissioned to do. There remains a difference between charism and office, between person and function.

Understood in this way, the notion of an "indelible character" is not the embodiment of a "metaphysical clericalism"; rather, it bears witness to the fact that the priestly office is not something in and for itself, that it is a function of service on behalf of others. Thus, because of the "objective" mission involved, the function of this office cannot depend on the subjective holiness of the officeholder. If it did, there would be too much uncertainty about salvation in the Church, and the priestly office, carrying too much weight of its own, would obscure the fact that the one and only priest is Jesus Christ himself.

---

[6] E. Schillebeeckx, *Christus: Sakrament der Gottbegegnung* (Mainz, 1960), pp. 61ff. On the sacramental character and its specific function in the sacraments of baptism, confirmation and orders, see E. Ruffini, "Character as a Concrete Visible Element of the Sacrament in Relation to the Church," in *Concilium* 31 (1968), pp. 101-114; for further reading, see footnote 8 of that article.

The Functions of the Priestly Office

The function of community leadership is carried out in a variety of individual functions, which flow organically from the one main task of serving the unity of the Church. The unity of the Church becomes operative concretely in the unity of our profession of the faith, in the unity of the eucharistic celebration (toward which all the other sacraments are oriented), and in the unity of our fraternal, communal ministry of love. Since these are the three principal manifestations of Church unity, the priestly office is particularly oriented around the ministry of the Word, the ministry of the sacraments (particularly the eucharist), and the ministry of fraternal service to one another.

The Church is, first and foremost, the community of those who have been called together through faith in the Word of God—i.e., it is the *congregatio fidelium*. The Church is assembled through the Word and in our communal profession of the faith. The ministry of the Word is a priestly ministry (Rom. 15, 16). Like the sacraments, the Word does not simply speak about grace and redemption; it also effects what it says (Is. 55, 11; 1 Thess. 2, 13; Heb. 4, 12). It is the *verbum efficax* which has given rise to the Church. The ministry of the Word is something which falls to all Christians; thus qualified lay people may be entrusted with the *missio catechetica* and the *missio homiletica*. But here again the ecclesiastical office exercises a directive function, seeking to preserve the unity of the Church in its witness to Christ and its profession of faith. Thus it has a teaching office, which is quite distinct from the teaching office of theologians. It is an office of vigilance, designed to serve the unity of the Church (Acts 20, 28; 1 Tim. 5, 17; 6, 3ff; 6, 12. 20; 2 Tim. 1, 8. 13; 2, 14ff; 4, 1ff; Tit. 1, 9ff).

The Church, assembled in the one faith, is realized most concretely and solidly in the unity of the eucharistic celebration. The eucharist is, in a very special way, the sign and symbol of unity (1 Cor. 10, 17). Thus the priestly office, serving the unity of the Church, is authorized to preside over the eucharistic celebration; there is a close connection between the priestly ministry and the eucharist (DS 1764; 1771). The special ministry of the priest in the eucharistic celebration becomes clearer and more understandable when we view it in the light of his ministry on behalf of Church unity. When we realize and appreciate the close tieup between the body of Christ which is the Church and the body of Christ in the eucharist, there is little danger that priestly consecration will be erroneously viewed in magical terms.

If we keep this fundamental tieup in mind, we find it easier to approach a solution to some borderline questions. History indicates that there have been instances when "non-ordained" people pronounced the eucharistic prayer (1 Cor. 14, 16; Did. 10, 7). While we cannot simply write this off as a perversion, we can see that the priestly office does have official responsibility for the eucharistic assembly and its unity. This being the case, a eucharistic celebration in opposition to the priestly office would be absurd and contrary to the very nature of the eucharist. What should be a sign and symbol of unity would be turned into an expression of dispute and contention.

The case is quite different, of course, in a critical situation where no priest has been available for a long time. Here the celebration of the eucharist by a non-ordained person would not symbolize defiance of the priestly office but sorrow over the people's separation from this office. If people in these circumstances assembled to commemorate the last will and testament of Jesus at the banquet table, then Christ certainly would be among them; there would be, at the very least, communion *in voto* with the Church and her priestly office. Would this be a eucharist in the strict sense of the word? This is a question which has not been discussed too much up to now. But it loses its edge when we realize that there can be various "degrees of solidity" in the celebration of the eucharist and various ways in which Christ may be present.[7]

Finally, the Church becomes a reality in the communal and reciprocal ministry of love. Here, too, the priestly office is empowered to further the unity of the community by its overall direction. This direction is not to be embodied in authoritarian

[7] *Decree on Ecumenism*, n. 22.

decrees and measures of brute force. On the contrary, it is meant to bring the various charisms into meaningful and fruitful contact with one another. It is meant to discover and awaken these charisms, to foster them and give them room to operate, while at the same time keeping them in their proper place and admonishing them when they endanger Church unity.

Because this integrating function of the priestly office is supposed to serve the unity and harmony of the Church, it fails in its duty if it becomes the occasion for strife in the Church. Of its very nature, then, the ecclesiastical office is collegially structured. Collegiality covers the relationship of bishops to each other, of all the bishops to the bishop of Rome, of priests to one another, and of all priests to their bishops.[8] It also covers the relationship between the charism of leadership and the other charisms in the Church. Vatican Council II's teaching on the episcopal office provides us with fundamental principles for the correct appreciation of the ecclesiastical office in general. Responsibility in the Church can only be carried out collegially, with the fullest possible collaboration and agreement from everyone. This rules out any and all autocratic forms of administration, and it calls for a "democratic" style in Church leadership; in other words, decision should follow upon the widest possible range of reflection and discussion.

Our attempt here has been to provide a new outlook on the priestly office, in terms of the function of community leadership. By no means did we intend to play off the pastoral office against the teaching office and the priestly office. On the contrary, our treatment anticipates these distinctions and shows how it is possible to integrate them into a reasonable whole once again.

This uniform picture of the priestly vocation persisted

[8] Here we cannot give a detailed treatment of the relationship between priest and bishop. Essentially it is to be viewed in the framework of the collegiality of the ecclesiastical office and in terms of the Church as *communio*. See B. Botte, "Presbyterium et ordo episcoporum," in *Irénikon* 29 (1956), pp. 5-27; *idem*, "Der Kollegialcharakter des Priester und Bischofsamtes," in *Das apostolische Amt*, ed. J. Guyot (Mainz, 1961), pp. 68-91; J. Ratzinger, "The Pastoral Implications of Episcopal Collegiality," *Concilium* 1 (1965), pp. 39-67.

throughout the first millennium of the Church's history. It was only in the second millennium of Church history that the priestly office, once viewed in functional terms, was accorded an intrinsic official power of authority unconnected with its ecclesial function.[9] It came to be viewed simply as the power of consecration (*potestas in corpus Christi eucharisticum*), and it was isolated from the ecclesial function of leading and unifying the Church (*potestas in corpus Christi mysticum*). The priestly power of consecration (in the narrow sense) was distinguished from the "power of jurisdiction". Only with Vatican Council II have we seen the first timid attempts to break through this chasm between *ordo* and *jurisdictio*,[10] a chasm which would have been unthinkable in the first thousand years of the Church's history and which has never been accepted in the Eastern churches.

The eucharist, insofar as it is the sign and symbol of Church unity, simply cannot be separated from the unity of the Church. Neither, then, can the power to celebrate the eucharist be separated from the power to lead the Church. The authoritative sacramental ministry of the priest can only be appreciated correctly if it is integrated once again with his ministry on behalf of the unity of the Church community.

If we try to understand the priestly ministry in terms of the function of community leadership and the duty of promoting Church unity, then we can also accord him a role in present-day society. For the unity of the Church is not closed in upon itself; it stands as a sign and a sacrament of the unity of the world.[11] The priestly ministry, then, involves a broader ministry on behalf of the peace and unity of mankind. It is closely tied up with one of the deepest and most pervasive longings of contemporary mankind.

[9] Y. Congar, *Für eine dienende und arme Kirche* (Mainz, 1965), pp. 43-46, 75-77.

[10] *Dogmatic Constitution on the Church*, n. 22 and the *nota explicativa praevia*, n. 2, with the commentary by J. Ratzinger, *Das Zweite Vatikanische Konzil* I (Freiburg-Basel-Vienna, 1966), pp. 352-54.

[11] *Dogmatic Constitution on the Church*, n. 9; *Pastoral Constitution on the Church in the Modern World*, n. 42.

Adrian Hastings/ *Tabora, Tanzania*

The Theological Problem of Ministries in the Church

It is axiomatic that there is a great difference between what can be said absolutely about the Church's ministry regardless of century and country—i.e., that it be in obedience to God, as known to us through the clear teaching of Scripture, the constant witness of tradition and the most authoritative declarations of the living Church from time to time—and the sociological pattern of ministry in any given time and place. There is no possible doubt that the latter can and should change vastly according to the diverse historical character of the world to which the Church must minister; equally, there is no doubt that it has so changed again and again. It would, then, be quite implausible, for example, to hold that the particular pattern on late medieval and Tridentine foundations which evolved in western Europe in the period 1815-1939 has any particular claim to be normative. Faced with the obvious truth (frequently referred to in Vatican Council II documents, notably the *Pastoral Constitution on the Church in the Modern World*) that human society is currently undergoing an unprecedented rapid period of change, it is clear *a priori* that this must entail very considerable changes in the sociological pattern of the Church's ministry.

The task of the present article is neither a theological study of the ministry and its many problems for its own sake, nor an examination of which structural changes could be necessary or

34

valuable today for the renewal of the ministry; instead its aim is simply to outline some theological conclusions that would seem particularly relevant as a basis for that renewal. It is clear that only those doctrinal positions can be "passed on" as a basis for pastoral renewal that are theologically more or less unquestionable. For example, it is held by some who have studied the ministry of the very early Church (H. Küng, in particular) that there were no "ordained" ministries in the early Pauline churches, that nonordained Christians presided at the eucharist in the first years of the Church of Corinth, and that "presbyters" were only introduced there later, after Paul's death. If such a position were to be accepted as certain, it might have very considerable practical implications. However, since this position is, in fact, historically and doctrinally questionable, it is not possible to make present use of it in reshaping our pattern of ministry.

This article will proceed by considering various issues which combine the theological content and current practical significance. Basic to the whole discussion is the recognition that the entire Church, the whole People of God, truly participates in the priesthood and mission given to all by Christ and communicated to each in baptism and confirmation; that the activation of this common participation is achieved in many ways, some of which are particular to certain individuals and which we call ministries; and that the shaping of the latter is achieved by God both through the known structures of the Church, hierarchically commissioned, and through the unpredictable inspiration of God in particular people and circumstances.

The International Ordering of the Threefold Ministry

A first theme concerns the internal ordering of the threefold commissioned ministry of bishops, presbyters and deacons. This pattern clearly emerged during the early dynamic years of the Church's growth. It was fixed before a hundred years had passed and it has basically remained ever since. This was reaffirmed by Chapter 3 of the *Dogmatic Constitution on the Church*. It would not be theologically acceptable to initiate pastoral reforms which did not respect this pattern, although it must be candidly admitted that in a great part of the Church the third category—the diaconate—was in fact atrophied for centuries (unless, indeed, the diaconate is ultimately to be interpreted as meaning every serious ministry of service in the Church, or at least every ministry that has been given some type of ecclesial commissioning— and such an interpretation is not impossible).

However, the acceptance of the commissioned ministry and its threefold shape has few precise implications as to how the ministry is structured in practice. It is clear that a collegial relationship both between and within the ministry of local churches is required, but this too can take many different forms. Theology has nothing decisive to say on such questions as whether a normal diocese will be a community with a ministry of ten presbyters or a thousand; it cannot settle whether a bishop should be the settled head of a small local church or an itinerant overseer of many local churches; it has nothing certain to offer as to whether a bishop is to be chosen by the laity of the local church, by its clergy, or by neighboring bishops, and the same is true at the level of the universal Church. In some way the bishop has to represent the local church within the world communion, just as he represents the total apostolic mandate at the local level, but various ways of selection and styles of life are honorably consistent with such requirements.

Again, while theology does suggest that the term "local church" refers at times most properly to something larger than a single diocese (to a province or patriarchate in fact), it cannot formulate the juridical character of such a unit or lay down what authority a local synod may have over the individual bishop, although it does say with certainty that there is and must be authority over the individual bishop, and there has always been so.

In the relationship of episcopate and presbyterate an important particular instance is provided by confirmation. The theology of this sacrament remains somewhat confused. Not the least part of this confusion is the nature of its relationship with the episcopal office. This relationship hardened in the Western

Church until it could be expressed almost dogmatically at Trent (Denz. 873). This ignored the Eastern experience which had moved in a contrary direction. It is well known that the early drafts of Vatican Council II's *Constitution on the Church* re-iterated the Tridentine formula that bishops were the "ordinary" ministers of confirmation. Confronted with the Eastern tradition, this was reformulated as "original ministers" (n. 26). In the same way the early drafts of the *Decree on the Catholic Churches of the Eastern Rite* equally affirmed that the bishop was the "sole ordinary minister of the sacrament of chrism". This was simply removed from the final document. The pastoral prac-tice of the Western Church was already noticeably modified in this matter by a decree of Pius XII in 1946. Today, theologically speaking, it is an entirely open matter whether in a local church the normal minister of confirmation be a presbyter or a bishop. Pastoral considerations must prevail. In a diocese with only a few thousand Christians, the normal retention of the bishop as minister may be a valuable way of maintaining a personal re-lationship between Christians and their chief local pastor. In a diocese of millions, the same retention may be a meaningless formality.

Here, as almost everywhere, the bishop-presbyter balance is, in principle, an extremely flexible one. Only as regards ordina-tion must current Catholic theology insist that, while the ques-tion is open for theological discussion, it is not at present open pastorally: ordinations to the presbyterate must be performed by a bishop. Elsewhere, in almost every case it can be that the final answer as regards the relating of bishops and presbyters in liturgy and sacrament, pastoral work, election and decision mak-ing, must depend upon the human and pastoral needs of the living Church, both local and universal.

Ordained and Non-Ordained Ministries

A second theme is that of the relationship between ordained and non-ordained ministries. It is clear that the earliest books of the New Testament present us with a rich diversity of ministries, and that at least some of these were clearly not associated with the laying on of hands. The contrast between the image of how a local church may be ordered as found in 1 Corinthians is strikingly different from that presented a good many years later by the pastorals. What is most certainly significant in the evidence of 1 Corinthians is its positive, not its negative, aspect. In fact, Acts also presents considerable evidence of a wide diversity of ministries. The pastorals and the letters of Ignatius suggest an impoverishment here: the "hierarchical" structure has somehow eaten up the other ministries (that, at least, is the impression they give). This could already easily point toward a Church wherein only a minority of members are really expected to exercise an active mission, just as (somewhat later) only a minority came to be expected to seek something described as "perfection" or, again, exercise their universal priesthood.

Vatican Council II has explicitly recognized that within the Church there is a variety of ministries (*Constitution on the Church*, n. 18; *Decree on the Apostolate of the Laity*, n. 2) corresponding to a variety of charisms. This is scripturally and theologically certain, and it is clear that the greater part of the activities normally associated with a priest's life in modern times can as fittingly be related to the non-ordained ministries: pastoral work of many kinds, teaching the faith to catechumens and to the young, visiting the sick, marriage counseling, administering church goods. In fact for many years such ministries have been regularly performed by catechists and nuns. What the basic theological relationship of these ministries is to the historic "diaconate" is not yet clear. The *Constitution on the Church* (n. 29) presents immediate pastoral guidance in a time of transition rather than a final doctrinal statement.

Historically it is clear that the tendency of the presbyteral ministry to "eat up" other ministries and consequently to create a rather clear division within the Church between ministers and those ministered to has been a repeated one. In subsequent centuries the tendency toward monoformity of the apostolic age has been repeated. In the 3rd and 4th centuries there was, for instance, a wide development of so-called "minor orders"—doorkeeper, exorcist, lector, acolyte. They grew up as what we can but call "lay ministries" suited to their times. Naturally lay ministries, when exercised publicly and continuously, need some measure of ecclesiastical recognition: their "order" must be seen in that light. But here again with the course of time these ministries came to be swallowed up into the presbyteral one. By the high Middle Ages the same fate, as regards the Western Church, had overtaken the diaconate. All became mere liturgical stepping stones to the priesthood.

The inherent need of a healthy Church for non-presbyteral ministries was, however, again manifested by the emergence of religious orders—monks, friars and nuns—whose male members were at first seldom intended to be ordained, or if they were, their type of ministry was viewed as strikingly different from that of the diocesan clergy. Here again, however, a leveling-out process quickly began to take place, transferring certain "religious" characteristics to the traditional clergy, but at the same time tending toward the ordination of all educated male religious. Modern pressures to obtain the ordination of teaching brothers may be viewed in this light.

Yet every time the pattern of a rather monolithic ministry has begun to emerge, new forces have appeared in an opposite direction. The modern lay apostolate movement can be seen in this way: new ministries emerging almost spontaneously here and there, but at the same time an almost instant reaction to try somehow to "discipline" this diversity—for instance, by allowing in a country a single "Catholic Action" movement (not actually presbyteral, yet defined as a participation in the hierarchy's apostolate, which is a very presbyteral conception).

Vatican Council II has affirmed the existence of a variety of charisms and the necessity for a plurality of ministries. Theology cannot state the concrete pattern these ministries should take at any particular moment, but it can state that they must not be conceived as all assimilable to the presbyterate either in the line of sacrament or in that of hierarchical direction. "The laity must not be deprived of the possibility of acting on their own accord" (*Decree on the Apostolate of the Laity,* n. 24)—a statement which indicates no more than the basic condition for a variety of fruitful ministries in the Church of God.

Segregation

A third theme of particular significance today is that of "segregation". This, too, is one of vast dimensions, which can be hardly more than indicated here. Its proper understanding is fundamental for New Testament thought and life, though it may take on different verbal forms. Christian life involves a total separation from sin, from the world, from the unclean, from the flesh (Rom. 6, 11-14; 7, 5-6; 8, 5-9; 12, 2; etc.). This separation or segregation is accomplished essentially by baptism—the sign of God's call—and its acceptance by man in faith. This separation and entering into the heritage of Christ is truly a "consecration", a making sacred or holy, and as a consequence Christians can be called "saints". But this Christian consecration is not a segregation from things or into places. Apart from withdrawal from activities held to be positively sinful, it has no sociological manifestation. There are not profane and sacred things, profane and sacred places. "The earth is the Lord's and everything in it" (1 Cor. 10, 26). "There is nothing outside a man which can defile him" (Mk. 7, 14). "Neither on this mountain nor in Jerusalem . . . but in spirit and in truth will you worship" (Jn. 4, 21-23). "What God has cleansed you must not call common" (Acts 9, 15). The problems of 1 Corinthians 8 and Romans 14 are expressed here: "We are no worse off if we do not eat, and no better off if we do" (1 Cor. 8, 8). Christian consecration and segregation do not involve going out from some activities or restricting oneself to some places. Baptism makes sacred but it finds the sacred in the created in its wholeness.

Clearly there is a special moment in Christian life which is in a unique way sacred and in which there was segregation from the start: the moment of the Lord's supper. Christians were set apart by that fact, and Paul's comparisons in 1 Corinthians 10 suggest that he saw it as somehow the Christian equivalent to Israelite and pagan sacred occasions. But it is clear that every Christian is equally involved in this type of "segregation" and its sacredness, and moreover that it somehow signifies the potential sacredness of everything else and hence of the non-segregation of all the rest of Christian life: "Whatever you do, do all for the glory of God" (1 Cor. 10, 31).

This common theology is really basic for a sound understanding of the ministry, because insofar as the Christian ministry may involve a particular "segregation", it still remains wholly of this theological type: a more intense concentration upon the Gospel of God, but not a sociological separation. Paul himself is the very type of it. He is "set apart for the Gospel of God"—segregation —but he remains a tentmaker, earning his living by selling his wares or his labor to unbelievers. This is basic to the theology of the ministry. We cannot go into here the complicated story of subsequent centuries, in which the sacred came too often to be seen as a recognizable sphere of life separable from the profane, and then as a sphere of life properly belonging to the ordained rather than to all Christians, and in which consecration for holiness also came to be seen rather as ordination or religious profession than as baptism. All of this gradually resulted in an outlook according to which priesthood was somehow incompatible with secular occupations. Such a view was never in fact fully implemented, but it has been constantly there in the background, from the time of St. Cyprian at least, to our own day—to declare from time to time that certain non-sinful human activities were nevertheless *per se* unsuitable for the priest. Theology must deny this, both on account of the New Testament evidence and from the intrinsic nature of the Christian economy.

Vatican Council II's *Decree on the Ministry and Life of Priests* stresses that the "segregation" required of the priesthood is a strictly theological one, not sociological (n. 3). Paul is taken as its explicit model. Hence the Decree goes out of its way to commend both the worker priest and the married priest (nn. 8, 16). Pastoral reasons may justify a priest either working for his living with his own hands or not doing so, either being married or not being married, but the theological nature of the Christian priesthood necessarily leaves such questions fully open.

The concept of a kind of sacredness of ordained ministers which requires for the sake of "congruity" their segregation from various lawful human activities, including marriage, seems inextricably bound up with an implicit clericalization of the Lord's supper and a clericalization, too, of the ideal of imitating Christ. It is not compatible with the New Testament understanding of consecration and the holy.

If the nature of the ordained ministry in no way rules out any non-sinful human activity for the minister, there is a consequent implication that, when all is said and done, theology has little to say about what proportion of a priest's time should be taken up by specifically ministerial functions, and, equally, how far he should be financially supported by the Church. In all ages there have been many priests, and good priests, the greater part of whose working life has been given to what can be listed as "secular" occupations, such as tentmaking, agriculture, the teaching in schools of non-religious subjects and historical research. The general principle that the Church should support her ministers depends in application upon the amount of time individual ministers give to explicit ministry, and the regulation of this depends again upon pastoral needs within a particular context, not on theology.

Celibacy

A fourth theme, already touched upon, is that of celibacy. It is scripturally and theologically certain that there is in the Church a charism of celibacy which provides a special witness to the kingdom and which can also greatly contribute to the effectiveness of many ministries. It is verified by Christian history that celibacy can be pastorally of great value, especially in the itinerant and missionary ministry. It is theologically certain that a Church faithful to the New Testament must make room for and encourage the acceptance of this charism, and that while it can equally fittingly be embraced by the non-ordained (including women!) it is also fitting that among men commissioned for the episcopal and presbyteral ministries this charism be widely found. However, it is also clear in principle, and can again be proved from Christian experience, that the conjunction in a single person of the sacraments of orders and matrimony is not only theologically permissible but pastorally valuable. Unless principles are to be applied in this field that are seriously different from those acceptable elsewhere in theology, it is impossible to build up any strong relationship between the ministerial priesthood and celibacy. Canonical practice in the greater part of the Church over a number of centuries can in no way be theologically decisive.

In this matter we have absolutely clear New Testament evidence. It is positive, not negative, guidance; moreover, it does not merely state facts but propounds what is suitable. Short of rejecting the pastoral epistles from the canon, theology can only accept the witness of 1 Timothy 3, 2-5 and Titus 1, 5-6. Here is a clear instance in which Western Catholics, accustomed to a particular ecclesiastical tradition, have to accept concretely Vatican Council II's message that the teaching office of the Church "is not above the Word of God, but serves it" (*Dogmatic Constitution on Divine Revelation,* n. 10). Furthermore, it is an historical fact—which theology cannot ignore—that there have been married Catholic priests carrying on a fruitful ministry in every single age of the Church from the 1st to the 20th century.

Theology, then, can only recognize the distinction between the charism of the ordained ministry and that of celibacy. It must recognize that both the linking in an individual life of the priesthood with celibacy and its linking with marriage have been providential in the order of history, both have scriptural foundation, and both can be pastorally fruitful.

Ministry as Service

The fifth and final theme is that which has in fact come to the fore in each of the preceding ones. The ministry is for the sake of

Church and mission, not the Church for the ministry. For instance, one cannot first of all posit an abstract "life and spirituality of priests" and then relate the conditions of the ministry to that life. The change in emphasis in the different drafts of Vatican Council II's *Decree on the Ministry and Life of Priests* is striking. The early drafts had tried to do just that: to lay down the holiness and life of priests first. The final Decree does the opposite: it starts with ministry. Ministry is service and service to someone; it is service, normally, within the context of a local church. The deepest nature of the New Testament ministry is just this: it is a *diakonia,* and the theological principle for its structuring is exactly that of relevance to the local fellowship and witness of the People of God in a particular space-time context.

Historically this is more or less what has happened, but it is also true that certain patterns of ministry have, especially in later times, become too rigid and have been maintained even when seriously unadapted to the *diakonia* of the People of God in a particular context. Many examples, especially from missionary history, can prove this with complete objectivity.

The *diakonia* of the ordained ministry has to provide the core of Word and sacrament for the Church, and that includes a regular eucharistic celebration for every real local community of baptized faithful. Any pattern for the ordained ministry which in a particular historical-social context seriously fails to do this must be condemned theologically. At the same time the pattern of the ordained ministry has to be such that it will stimulate rather than supplant a variety of other ministries in the Church —missionary, prophetic and those relating to social service—so that the calling of the whole Christian people with a diversity of charisms is assisted rather than suppressed, and the witness and communion of the whole Church, local and catholic, are effectively served in the changing world of history, geography and economics.

Emile Pin, S.J./*Rome, Italy*

The Priestly Function
in Crisis

Over the past three years there has been an increasing number of books and articles on the priest.[1] It is now hackneyed to talk about a "crisis in the Catholic priesthood". It is indeed a fact that many priests are openly giving up the priesthood, and that the number of candidates for the priesthood is diminishing somewhat everywhere. When the problems of the post-conciliar Church are being discussed, the question of the priest's role or function today comes up sooner or later.

The question is often raised in connection with the debate over obligatory celibacy. More and more frequently lay people and priests are questioning the grounds for this ecclesiastical law.[2] Among those who have studied the question, however, there seems to be a growing feeling that the repeal of this law alone will not resolve the present crisis. Obligatory celibacy itself, to be

[1] To mention a few recent titles: C.I.S.R., *Clergy in Church and Society*, 9th International Conference of the Sociology of Religion (Rome, 1967); Entr'aide Sacerdotale en Europe, *Le Prêtre et le monde sécularisé* 53 (Maastricht, 1968); I-DOC, *C'è un domani per il prete?* (Mondadori, 1968).

[2] A survey taken in Paris during 1967 showed the following results. 68% of those questioned felt that priests would fulfill their functions just as well (35.5%) or better (32.1%) if they were married. 15% were undecided. Only 17.6% (25% if you consider only habitually practicing Catholics) felt that married priests would perform their functions more poorly.

sure, does pose problems that deserve to be studied, especially when we consider the manner in which candidates are chosen, the moral pressures to which they are often subjected during the period of formation, and the age at which the definitive commitment is made.[3] Yet the core of the problem seems to be situated on a different level, involving the role—or, more precisely, the function—of the priest.[4] The celibacy crisis—or, more precisely, the present-day aspect of this crisis—appears to result from the fact that the priestly function has been called into question.

Apropos of the priest, people now talk about the man without a profession,[5] the perplexed profession,[6] or the priest's crisis of identity.[7] The priest, it seems, no longer knows who he is; the expectations of the faithful no longer give him a clear idea of

---

[3] The argument is often put forward that minor seminaries must exist, because if you do not get candidates while they are still young, they will lose their vocation. This suggests that the minor seminary can easily turn into a regime of moral pressure.

[4] "The many defections in the priesthood today are not rooted principally in difficulties relating to the sexual and emotional order (in the best sense of these words). It is my opinion that they result mainly from the priest's inability to pinpoint his own place and to find a solid commitment": A. Vergote, "Riflessioni psicologiche sul divenire umano del sacerdote," in *C'è un domani per il sacerdote?* (Mondadori, 1968), p. 217. "At first glance one might think that the major cause of this malaise is ecclesiastical celibacy. . . . But we find that Protestants are encountering almost the same difficulties: laxity and disquiet among their ministers, growing difficulty in recruiting ministerial candidates, etc. . . . The problem of malaise seems to be far more general and widespread than we might have imagined it to be at first. It would be a mistake or an alibi to relate it strictly to problems in the sexual life. As R. P. Beirnaert puts it, ecclesiastical celibacy is the point around which many deeper problems have crystallized": Marc Oraison, "Le débat sur le célibat des prêtres," in *Le Monde,* April 9, 1968, p. 1.

[5] Marc Oraison, "Le prêtre: un homme sans métier?" in *Christus* 48 (1965), pp. 462-75.

[6] Luchesius Smits ("Sacerdoti per una società nuova," in *C'è un domani per il prete?* p. 175) applies to priests the observations of Reinhold Niebuhr on the Protestant minister. According to Niebuhr (*The Purpose of the Church and Its Ministry* [New York, 1956], p. 28), the Protestant ministry is a "perplexed profession" (R. H. Niebuhr).

[7] "Today it is almost a truism to talk about the priest losing his image or his identity, or to say that he is desperately seeking a new, updated image": Pierre Fransen, "Quelques remarques dogmatiques sur le sacerdoce chrétien," in *Le prêtre et le monde sécularisé,* p. 37.

what he should be and what he should do. Many priests feel that they are no longer of any use as priests. We might sum up their feelings and their doubts by saying that the priestly function no longer confers the status—that is, the prestige, the power and the recognition—that was once attached to it.

In this article we shall try to explain why. We shall first examine the roots of the present crisis and the various priestly reactions to it. Then we shall offer a new outlook on the priestly function—or, better, on the priestly *functions,* for are we not seeing a gradual splitting up of what used to be a single, uniform function?

Priestly Status in a Changing World

The power of the priest has been undergoing diminution for quite a long time. Outside small farming villages in rural areas, *the priest is no longer the central figure in the local community,* and the community itself is in a process of radical change. The sacral character of traditional farming communities invested priests with powers and privileges which were rooted in his ritual and ethical functions and extended from there to all the domains of human existence.

The process of rationalization and specialization and the resultant secularization have gradually gnawed away at the priest's power and privileges in society. People refuse to listen to him in the domains that are not his own. He no longer has the power to directly regulate the life of the community and the individual. His power is now indirect: that is, it is limited to those who freely put themselves under it, and to the realm of ethics and ritual.

Even this indirect power is now menaced, for within the community of the faithful there is a growing tendency to question the priest's competency on ethical questions. The various aspects of everyday life (economics, politics, literature, art, etc.), over which he once exerted some indirect influence at least, are now operating entirely outside his control. Confined to the sacristy and the confessional, and not participating in the specialized functions of our present societal life, he is finding it harder and harder to understand and to guide consciences. His counsels and his judgments are often off the mark, revealing his ignorance rather than his competence.[8]

This process of transformation, which was going on throughout the last century, *has reached its climax in our day,* and it is only in recent years that we have seen the full psychological repercussions. Even when the priest was aware of his social impotence in the past, even when he realized his incompetence in the field of ethics, he could still console himself with the performance of his ritual functions. He might not contribute to the building up of the world by direct action or by spiritual counseling, but he would be able to save souls by administering the sacraments.

Solidly grounded on the dogma of *ex opere operato,* he made every effort to see to it that the faithful would devote some time each week to their religious duties, no matter how much frivolity and materialism infected their daily work. Many artifices helped to ensure frequent reception of the sacraments, and everyone's absolute confidence in their efficacity reassured both priest and faithful. Moreover, the confidence of the faithful helped to convince the priest that his work, however irrelevant in this world, surely had some usefulness for the world to come.

Vatican Council II has shaken these convictions. The major shock seems to have come from the *liturgical reform* and the *Pastoral Constitution on the Church in the Modern World.* Without challenging or questioning the essentials of sacramental theology, the liturgical reform accords a primordial importance to the active role of the faithful in the sacramental celebration. The faithful must use their intellect and will; they must understand the language and the symbols; they must participate. The important thing is the interior revitalization that takes place in them, and that must be manifested outwardly in a better way of life. Some even go so far as to say that man's real worship of God

---

[8] When a poll was being taken in a diocese of northern Italy, a recurrent complaint was that priests are not equipped to understand the problems that people run up against in everyday life.

is not the worship he renders in Church but his manner of behaving in daily life.

The *Pastoral Constitution on the Church in the Modern World* goes on to suggest that the Church is only fully herself when she is in contact with the world, and that she must incessantly work at moving the world toward a more perfect form of justice. In the long run, what counts is not the sacred rite but the charity which comes from God and animates the concrete happenings of daily life.

This shift in emphasis within the Church seems to be the ultimate factor responsible for the present crisis with regard to the priestly function. It appears to have destroyed the last line of psychological resistance. Previously, the priest could console himself over his loss of power in the social arena by noting that he was saving souls through the administration of the sacraments. Now suddenly he is given to understand that such salvation is effected only in the heart of the world itself, and only through the concrete happenings of our overall existence.

The Reactions of Priests

We can discern three basic reactions on the part of priests. First, a large number of priests are living out their life on the margin of the Council.[9] They calmly go about their ritual functions as before, supported by a large number of faithful who still live in the dualistic (sacred versus profane) framework of a bygone age. This attitude, understandably enough, is found most frequently among older priests. A second group of priests is unable to see how they can reconcile the new religious vision with the routine pastoral tasks imposed on them by tradition, their elders and their flock. Finally, a third group of priests hopes to effect this reconciliation; within the framework of their priestly role, they are trying to adapt to the new orientations of the postconciliar Church.

There is not much to say about the first category of priests.

[9] A rapid poll taken among the priests of one diocese in Italy revealed that only 10% of the clergy had taken note of the conciliar documents.

Their inability to understand what is going on among "young people" in the Church, their happy or tortured ritualism, and their resistance to pastoral *aggiornamento* reinforce the conviction of priests in the second category that "nothing can be done" within the bosom of the institutional Church.

This second group of priests—those who abandon the ministry—deserve more detailed study that we can provide here. It is probable that behind their defection lies a whole series of motives that cannot easily be disentangled from one another. But let us try to sketch their situation in brief fashion.

On the surface it would seem that the constraints imposed on the priest—obedience and celibacy, in particular—are too much for many of these priests. But were these constraints that much easier to take in the past? It would seem that these constraints were easier to put up with in the past because they seemed to be necessary to the carrying out of the priestly task, a task judged to be essential by the community. Now, however, spirituality has taken a different turn: stress is being put on concrete existence instead of on rite, the spiritual significance of the sexual relationship has been rediscovered, and personal responsibility is being given emphasis over obedient submissiveness. As a result, obedience and chastity have lost some of their witness value and their functional utility.

Moreover, while society still has need of rites, they now are regarded as being of secondary importance. The priest is a useful person, but many other functions are regarded as more useful. Even the most faithful Christians are beginning to question the priest's monopoly in sacramental functions.[10] Many practicing faithful do not seem to receive the sacraments to achieve the

---

[10] This questioning can find some support in Church history. "In the course of history, lay people have baptized, conferred extreme unction, distributed holy communion, and heard confessions—sacramental or not. It is high time for us to reintroduce into our sacramental theology the notion of 'economy', which is still quite alive in the Eastern rites": Pierre Fransen, "Quelques remarques dogmatiques sur le sacerdoce chrétien," in *Le Prêtre et le monde sécularisé*, p. 49. The author's conclusion is that it is not necessary to establish an absolute and fixed line of demarcation between the competencies of the faithful and those of the priest.

purpose for which they were instituted. Instead, they go simply to fulfill a ritual obligation that binds them under pain of serious sin. Finally, the majority of baptized persons in many countries could hardly be called real believing Christians;[11] they attend the key rites—baptism, first communion, confirmation, marriage and the burial service—because they coincide with major events in their societal or personal lives.

The priest who knows the real meaning of the sacraments refuses to become the mere agent of certain social functions. He was not made a priest to be that, and these functions do not justify the obligations he has taken on with ordination. If the demands of his superiors and of the faithful do not allow him to dedicate a major part of his time to some profane or religious activity that ties in with the proclamation of the Gospel, then he would prefer to leave the ministry.[12]

The third group of priests seeks to implement the new goals of the post-conciliar Church within their own sacerdotal ministry. This is relatively easy for those who are free from the social constraints mentioned above, and who are able to exercise their ministry in a priestly brotherhood and a community of believers that are truly Christian, sincerely trying to implement the will of God in their daily lives. Here the expectations of the faithful sustain him in his ministry, helping him to bear the burdens of poverty, celibacy and obedience even when he does not see their clear justification.

Not all priests, however, find themselves in this fortunate position. Even when they do, there are still difficulties to be faced. The first difficulty is the absence of a ready-made model defining

---

[11] In the Paris poll cited earlier, only 38% of those baptized held the divinity of Christ as certain, but the vast majority (from 80% to 85%) intended to have their children baptized, to have them receive first holy communion, and to get Christian burial themselves. Among those who wanted Christian burial, only 22% said that they firmly believed in the resurrection.

[12] The reason advanced for leaving the ministry may well be a rationalization of more individualistic motives. But the fact that it can be advanced at all suggests the new outlook prevailing among the clergy and the faithful.

the role of the post-conciliar priest in a secularized society. A new model must be constructed, but on what basis? The second difficulty is getting this new model accepted by the hierarchy and the faithful.

The Priestly Role in the Past

A role is a complex of models which society as a whole or a particular group imposes on an individual who wishes to perform a determined function in their midst. If the individual conforms to the behavior models that they expect of him, he is recompensed by the group.

In the traditional society of the past,[13] in which the role of the priest gradually took on the definition that prevailed up to our own day, most of the functions (particularly those involving authority) were assigned to people by right of birth or by virtue of some sort of sacred investiture. Both types of assignation were felt to bestow on the individual an essentially different character; by virtue of this character, the individual acquired a certain "power" and the right to demand obedience from others. The power and the concomitant right were not granted by the group by virtue of some specific and demonstrated competence, but by virtue of a character that was "innate" or, at the very least, invested in the core of his personality. This character conferred a "universal" or "general" competence on the king, the nobleman and the priest.

In the case of the priest, this investiture was tied up with his ordination—that is, with the power conferred on him by the Church to celebrate the eucharist and certain other sacraments. By virtue of this fundamental capacity, the priest received from the group a mission and certain powers, rights and privileges relating to everything which directly or indirectly touched upon the sacred. He sacralized various familial, local and national events. He preached the Gospel, taught theology and the catechism, and gave instruction in moral law and philosophy. He

[13] This term does not apply solely to a society of the past, but to any society where tradition is the norm of truth and decision.

also supervised schools, counseled people in spiritual, psychological and pedagogical matters, and administered various persons and properties in the Church in the name of the faithful.

The priest did not get any specialized training to handle these many and varied functions. He was no better prepared to exercise authority than the rest of his contemporaries. The idea was simply to make a "good" man out of him.

In the course of the last two centuries, however, the arts and crafts and sciences have become specialized. The principle of competence has replaced the principle of investiture, and the notion of universal competence is now ruled out. Even if one admits that the "power of orders" is associated with an investiture that is of a different nature than scientific competence, one no longer sees it as the source of all sorts of diversified competence in the Church or in society. Such special competence presupposes a long period of specialized training and the practical exercise of it in some permanent way.[14]

That is why many young priests today feel ill-equipped for the tasks they are assigned. They point an accusing finger at the seminary and the university.[15] But what school could give its students training in such a wide variety of specialized fields? Perhaps the real fault lies not with the seminary, but with the fact that the priestly task has not been differentiated clearly enough. As of now, the priest's work seems to be an impossible conglomerate of widely varying functions, for which no academic curriculum could prepare him properly. Selectivity and specialization seem to be called for.

The necessity for choosing some specialty raises several problems. To begin with, it would be necessary to define certain roles distinctly and precisely enough so that adequate formation in

[14] Most of the modern specializations begin with training in school, but they are truly acquired by effective daily exercise of them.

[15] These institutions can only be reformed if they first develop a clear idea of their real aims and goals. Unfortunately, professors are probably to be included with those who are least in contact with the changes that are taking place in the Church and in society. They are better at maintaining a tradition than at understanding a transformation.

them could be envisaged. If we do this, we may find that the traditional link between the power of orders (the priestly function in the strict sense) and certain other ecclesiastical functions is not a necessary one at all. A consequence of this would be that the methods of selecting candidates, the age of entering upon the priestly career, and the obligations and rewards offered could no longer be the same as they were; they would have to vary in accordance with each function.

Priestly Functions Today and Tomorrow

Here we shall briefly analyze the principal functions, now included in the priestly task, which would have to be split up and clearly differentiated in the future.

We have already mentioned the task of *blessing or consecrating events in the life of the family, the local community and the nation:* baptism, funeral services, national parades, house blessings, etc. Younger members of the clergy have evinced great repugnance for this function, especially since Vatican Council II. They do not feel that their ordination, which is centered around the eucharistic mystery and which makes them bearers of a universal, prophetic hope, should also make them civic functionaries of this type.[16] It does indeed seem that this function is on its way out.

A second traditional function of the priest in most religions is his role as *an intermediary between God and the faithful in obtaining favors.* This function is also repugnant to the younger generation of priests. Rightly or wrongly, they feel that it makes sorcerers and medicine men out of them.

Having ruled out these two functions, now rejected by the new orientations of the Church, we can spell out some of the functions that are still acceptable today but that may need clearer

---

[16] The mythical character of the civic-centered priesthood seems to require that it be exercised by men endowed with preternatural powers. These powers are vouched for by their strange habits and dress, by social separation and by sexual taboos. None of this helps to clarify the already difficult problem of celibacy.

differentiation. In the Catholic Church of the Latin rite, almost all the *theologians* are priests. All priests receive a long period of academic formation in the theological sciences. In the Greek Orthodox Church, by contrast, a theologian is usually a layman.

Now there does not seem to be any necessary link between the two functions. Is there any good reason why the present obligations attached to the priestly function must be imposed on the theologian? Offhand, there does not seem to be. To be sure, the Church (i.e., the community of the faithful and the hierarchy) could continue to invite certain theologians into the priesthood and episcopate if they had the proper qualifications for these latter functions, and it would be not only permissible but also quite reasonable for a theologian to be a religious as well. In any case theology is a developed discipline requiring a long career of academic study; like any other academic career of this type, it should be entered into while the candidate is still young.[17]

Traditionally the priest has been a *counselor*. At one time his counseling touched upon many domains of life, but gradually it has been restricted to the religious domain. Today both priests and laymen have been made aware of the difficulties of spiritual counseling by several factors: a changing outlook on the nature and meaning of religious activity, the discovery of the intricate psychological roots underlying religious attitudes and motivations, and the growth of a more existential concept of morality and human conduct. Today the counselor must have not only religious conviction, but also personal maturity and a deep psychological formation.

These attributes are only acquired with growth in years and specialized study. A one- or two-semester course in psychology

[17] Alongside the function of the theologian proper, there are the various complementary functions of religious education. Very few priests today receive the proper formation, particularly the pedagogic formation, to carry out these functions adequately. In the Italian poll mentioned earlier, several people suggested that it would be more worthwhile to entrust religious instruction to qualified lay teachers than to priests. Students do in fact prefer to speak to their lay teachers about religion rather than to priests.

will not equip our seminarians to handle the task of counseling adequately. This counseling function would seem to be suitable for certain religious, provided that they maintain systematic contact with the problems of contemporary men and women. But there does not seem to be any necessary tieup between counseling and the sacerdotal function itself. Here again, of course, there would be nothing to prevent a particular spiritual counselor from being called to ordination.

The same remarks would hold true for people who pursue other ecclesiastical careers: e.g., canon lawyers, specialists in various technical and human disciplines, and administrators. Some specialized formation is required for such work, the length of time involved depending on the importance and difficulty of the task itself. The length and complexity of the required study period, among other things, would suggest at what general age one should enter upon these careers. There would be a difference, for example, between a career that was more or less strictly ecclesiastical and a career that was little more than a slight variation on a secular career. Here again the idea is gaining ground that such functions have no necessary tieup with the sacerdotal function, the episcopal function or the religious state.

The three functions mentioned above (theologian, counselor, ecclesiastical functionary) presuppose faith, aptitude, competence and a vocation (in the broad sense of that word). The function of *apostle or missionary,* on the other hand, does not depend on scholarly or scientific competence first and foremost. It presupposes a charism, a vocation (in the strict sense of that word). One cannot allege that an apostle must always be a priest or a bishop—St. Paul himself distinguishes his mission from that of the *presbyters*—but the habitual obligations imposed on the priest do seem to fit in with the requirements of prophetic witness and the functional demands of the apostolic vocation.

Vocation, charism, serious studies (scriptural studies in particular) and total dedication seem to be normal conditions of an apostolic mission. The age for taking on a final commitment here should be more advanced than that required for the functions mentioned above, especially if a man is being asked to take on a definitive dedication and celibacy.[18]

The *strictly sacerdotal function,* that of priests and bishops, seems to involve one essential function: presiding over Christian communities. Tied up with this function is the celebration of the eucharist.[19] It seems that such a task does not require scholarly or scientific competence as the principal prerequisite, but rather sufficient experience to direct and unify the community.

Here we are talking about spiritual experience, his practical example of a life based on faith, broad human experience enabling him to understand his people, and group experience that would allow him to preside over the exchanges within his community and serve as a center of unity. In the light of these requirements, a growing number of commentators feel that the Church will not choose her future priests and bishops from among adolescents or even young adults. The tendency will be to choose men at a more mature stage of life. Priests will be chosen from every profession (including the ecclesiastical professions mentioned above), and simple priestly ordination will not involve the renunciation of their previous profession or of its exercise. If a priest is then called to assume some more important function (e.g., the episcopate), he may well have to give up his earlier profession and acquire a deeper theological and pastoral formation.

Such are the broad outlines now taking shape in the minds of many. The splitting up of the priestly function is merely one more example of the specialization process that is general in our day.

At the Crossroads

To say that this evolution is possible and desirable does not mean that it will involve no difficulties. The role open to indi-

[18] Antoine Vergote feels that ordination should not be conferred before a person has reached the age of 27 or 28 ("Réflexions psychologiques sur le devenir humain et chrétien du prêtre," in *Le prêtre et le monde sécularisé,* p. 77).

[19] Here we shall not take up the theological question of the tieup existing between these two functions.

vidual selection does not depend solely on personal choice. There must be a group who sees its need for the function chosen, sanctions it psychologically and materially, and approves the ways in which it is exercised. There is a wide range of people who have recourse to the services of the priest—from the higher echelons of the hierarchy to baptized people who are not practicing Catholics at all. It is quite possible that only a few groups or a small handful of individuals would be disposed to sanction the new restructuring and its concomitant specialization.

Today the priestly function is at the crossroads. It is being subjected to various pressures and tensions which, it seems, can only be resolved by clarifying and splitting up what used to be a monolithic function. The one function must become many functions. Each function must be tied up with a specific aim and purpose, each role must be defined, the various requirements must be determined, and the process of formation must be set up accordingly.

The question facing the Church as a whole—that is, her hierarchy and her faithful—is simply this: Is she ready to read the signs of the times and to study the problem while she still has thousands of priests in her service, or will she sit back and wait until the problem has taken on the proportions of a major crisis?

Frans Haarsma/*Nijmegen, Netherlands*

The Presbyterium: Theory or Program for Action?

Vatican Council II handled the concept of collegiality with evident though limited success not only in its reassessment of the episcopal office but also in its application to the priests as the bishop's collaborators.[1] More than in the case of the bishops where the idea maintained itself longer in practice and was earlier revived as a theory, the effect on the priests depends on the question whether the implications can be made operative and lead to changes in structure. This article hopes to make here a modest contribution to this end. After a brief glance back in retrospect, the idea of the presbyterium will be critically examined, and I shall conclude with a few thoughts about pastoral work as a whole.

I

THE PRESBYTERIUM IN RETROSPECT

Too little work has been done in Church history in the field of pastoral work to provide us with a more or less responsible sur-

---

[1] The term "presbyterium" occurs in the *Constitution on the Church* (n. 28), the *Decree on the Renewal of Religious Life* (n. 14), the *Decree on the Ministry and Life of Priests* (nn. 7-8), the *Decree on the Pastoral Office of Bishops in the Church* (nn. 11, 15, 28), and the *Decree on the Apostolate of the Laity* (nn. 19-20). The *Synopse des Textes Conciliaires* (ed. J. Deretz and A. Nocent, Paris, 1966) is not complete in its reference in this case as in others.

vey of the history of the presbyterium precisely as a "college". We must therefore limit ourselves to the recent past, which is still the present in many dioceses and has not yet reached the past tense in any. But before discussing the question whether and how the idea of collegiality has functioned until now, we must for a moment return to the most important historical source to which we owe, if not the term, at least the idea of the presbyterium as a collegial entity—namely, the letters of Ignatius of Antioch.[2]

The Presbyterium in the Letters of Ignatius of Antioch

In theological literature the presbyterium of Antioch often figures as the ideal image over against which the actual relationships in the average diocese today stand in sharp contrast. A strong and intimate bond with a mystical slant exists between the bishop and the presbyterium. This relationship is not one of equality, for the presbyterium is subject to the bishop as the apostles were to the Father. On the other hand, however, priests share in the bishop's authority so that the community owes the same obedience to both. The college of priests is the bishop's senate and shares with him the responsibility for the well-being of the ecclesial community. Bishop and presbyterium are therefore two-in-one, inseparable and indivisible, as the strings of the zither form one whole with the instrument itself (Eph. 4, 1). The obedience of the priests and the authority of the bishop are lifted to the level of a higher unity of love by a supernatural bond. This common bond with the bishop is at the same time the principle of unity among the members of the presbyterium.

[2] J. Lecuyer, "Le presbyterium," in J. Frisque and Y. Congar, *Les Prêtres. Formation, ministère et vie* (Paris, 1968), pp. 275-88; J. Pascher, "The Relation between Bishop and Priests," in *Concilium* 2 (1965), pp. 25-32; B. Botte, "Caractère collégial du presbytérat et de l'épiscopat," in *Etudes sur le sacrement de l'ordre* (Paris, 1957), pp. 97-124; *idem*, "The Collegial Character of the Priesthood and the Episcopate," in *Concilium* 4 (1965), pp. 184-94; J. Colson, *Les fonctions ecclésiales aux deux premiers siècles* (Paris, 1956); *idem*, "Le rôle du presbyterium et de l'évêque dans le contrôle de la liturgie chez S. Ignace d'Antioche et le rôle de Rome au second siècle," in *Paroisse et Liturgie* 47 (1965), pp. 15-24; J. Giblet, "Die Priester 'Zweiten Grades'," in G. Baraúna, *De Ecclesia II* (Freiburg, 1966), pp. 189-213; H. von Campenhausen, *Kirchliches Amt und geistliche Vollmacht* ([2] 1963), pp. 105-16.

However important the principles which this picture allows us to deduce for the pastoral structures of a diocese, it *cannot* serve as an *operational* model. This is already obvious from the plain fact that Ignatius' letters contain no accurate indication whatever about the way the presbyterium actually functioned in Antioch.

Reasons for the Factual Disappearance of Collegiality

If we look at our recent past, we can only say that little remained even of Ignatius' *idea* of collegiality. The relations between bishop and priests in the recent past can only be called frankly *juridical* and *hierarchical*. The element of a mystical bond may well still linger in *particular liturgical customs,* such as concelebration at a priest's ordination, but even there it was overshadowed by the hierarchical distance between bishop and priests. In the matter of administration, some remains, like the *diocesan synod* and *pro-synod,* passed through the same process, sharply expressed in Canon Law which says that "the one and only legislator in the synod is the bishop; all others only have a consultative voice; he alone signs the decisions of the synod" (Can. 362). Although the names of "senate" and "council" are still used for the *chapter* (Can. 391), it has lost most of the theological meaning of a presbyterium by the limits imposed on its competence as well as by the bishop's exclusive right to appoint its members. As to the rest of the priests, particularly those directly involved in pastoral care, they are seen, and see themselves, as men who *carry out the decisions* of the episcopal curia or the Roman authorities, decisions with which they have had nothing to do.[3]

The mutual relations between the ordinary priests constitute a pattern of apparently contradictory elements. There is first of all the hierarchical and juridical position of the parish pastor toward the curate, which has frequently caused curates to remain in a position of marked dependence in the execution of their pastoral function far into their middle age. At the same time the clergy as

---

[3] Cf. O. Schreuder, *Het professioneel karakter van het kerkelijk ambt* (Nijmegen, 1964); *idem,* "Le caractère professionel du sacerdoce," in *Social Compass* 12 (1965), pp. 5-19.

a group show a strong homogeneity, based on the basic equality in spiritual power, derived from the sacrament of orders. The sacramental-liturgical aspect of the priesthood has been stressed so one-sidedly that differences in character and professional ability played only a small part in the pastoral position or status. This same limited view of the nature of the priestly function, together with the conviction that every priest represented Christ and distributed his grace in virtue of his sacerdotal character, encouraged, on the other hand, a far-reaching *individualism,* not infrequently combined with a certain mutual competitiveness in pastoral work. If one adds to this the shared seminary education for a number of years, retreats in groups, recreation almost exclusively within their own circle, the living together in the rectory and the great social prestige bestowed on them by lay people who were for the greater part inarticulate, one can see that this adds up to the kind of *clericalism* which also determined the relations of the group toward those outside.

This quick sketch obviously is a generalization and lacks all the finer points. It is also limited by the restricted experience of the author which does not extend very far beyond the situation in Holland. In spite of these reservations, however, it may serve as a starting point for the discussion of how the concept of collegiality, revived by Vatican Council II, can be put into practice.

II
SHOULD WE RESTORE THE PRESBYTERIUM?

*The Impossibility of Restoring
the Presbyterium of the Old Church*

I have already pointed out that the concept of the presbyterium as found in Ignatius of Antioch provides no model for new pastoral structures. I would like to go further and ask whether the basic ideas which prevail in the present Church are still viable, since it seems to me that this is only partly true. To start with, the ideal of a restored presbyterium under one bishop and serving one community is unrealistic, whether we look at vast but thinly populated dioceses or at smaller dioceses with a hundred thousand souls or more. If we wish to seriously consider the restoration of the presbyterium in the old ecclesiastical sense, we can only do so by going back to the system of city bishops: every dean and subdean in the larger cities should be a bishop, while the present bishops should become metropolitans charged with the organization and coordination of affairs which cover wider regions and with maintaining contact with the other parts and the center of the Church.[4] For the time being, the difficulty of a still more complicated bureaucracy and of still more obstacles to an efficient and proportional distribution of the clergy seems to outweigh the possible advantages.

The Presbyterium Understood in an "Ontological" and "Mystical" Sense

We must add to this that the necessary differentiation between the Church's officials would encounter still greater difficulties, particularly in the field of non-territorial pastoral care. Finally, one may wonder whether the pronounced mystical bond which lies at the root of this idea still fits in with the present more functional image of the Church. Particularly the "father-son" relationship, applied to the relationship between bishop and priest in some conciliar documents, seems theologically exaggerated and psychologically unsuitable. The Council itself shows some hesitations on this point, for it maintains the elements of "bond" as well as "dependence" in this relationship. The "bond" lies in the common functional charism, the participation in Christ's priesthood: "The priests . . . are united with the bishops in sacerdotal dignity. By the power of the sacrament of orders, and in the image of Christ, the eternal high priest, they are consecrated to preach the Gospel, shepherd the faithful, and celebrate divine worship as true priests of the New Testament. . . . The priests, prudent cooperators with the episcopal order . . .

[4] Cf. H. Küng, *Die Kirche* (Freiburg, 1967), pp. 507-08.

constitute one presbyterium with their bishop." [5] Their dependence is sometimes put forward as an ontological one where the priests share in what the bishops possess in full: "On account of this sharing in *his* priesthood and mission, let priests sincerely look upon the bishop as their *father,* and reverently obey him. And let the bishop regard his priests, who are his co-workers, as *sons* and friends, *just as* Christ called his disciples no longer servants but friends." [6] "In consequence, they form one priesthood and one family, whose father is the bishop." [7]

It is part of this image that the priests "make the bishop present in a certain sense in the individual local congregations of the faithful, and take upon themselves, as far as they are able, his duties and his concerns, discharging them with daily care"; [8] in this sense they may also be called the "organs" of the bishop.[9] This dependence is seen at the same time as *functional:* the task and mission to be fulfilled require a cooperation in which the priests accept the guidance of the bishop. The latter need not exclude the former, but one may say that it is a logical conclusion. But it is equally true that the latter does not necessarily presuppose the former. The ontological view of dependence can also be an exaggerated ideological argument to reinforce the indispensable authority of the bishop.

That this was felt to some degree at Vatican Council II seems likely from the following facts. First of all, certain original formulations which firmly pointed in this direction were dropped in the final draft. These are the sentence "The bishops ordain the priests . . . over whom they let flow abundantly the grace of their own fullness" [10] and the phrase "true priests *of the second degree*".[11] It is also noticeable that the last conciliar document, the

[5] *Constitution on the Church,* n. 28.
[6] *Ibid.*
[7] *Decree on the Pastoral Office of Bishops in the Church,* n. 28.
[8] *Constitution on the Church,* n. 28.
[9] *Ibid.*
[10] Cf. A. Grillmeier, "Das Zweite Vatikanische Konzil," in *L.Th.K.* II (Freiburg, 1966), pp. 253-54.
[11] H. Küng (*op. cit.,* pp. 506-07) points out that there was no desire to solve the question about the dogmatic distinction between the functions of

Decree on the Ministry and Life of Priests, deals far more discreetly with this point. It is true that here the priests are exhorted "to keep in mind the fullness of the sacrament of orders which the bishop enjoys [and to] respect in him the authority of Christ, the chief shepherd" (n. 7), but there is no mention of a "father-son" relationship nor is the term "organ" employed. The "sons and friends" of the *Constitution on the Church* (n. 28) has become "brothers and friends" in the *Decree on the Ministry and Life of Priests* (n. 7), and apart from being collaborators who must obey, they are now also "counselors" to whom the bishop should "gladly listen" and with whom "he must discuss those matters which concern the necessities of pastoral work and the welfare of the diocese" (*ibid.*).

The line of development that was already indicated at Vatican Council II should be pursued if we wish to restructure pastoral work in the diocese. It offers a better perspective than a mere return to the old presbyterium because it is more factual and functional.[12]

III

INTEGRATED PASTORAL WORK

*The Function of the Priests' Council
and the Pastoral Council in a Diocese*

A diocesan "senate of priests" or priests' council, as suggested by the *Decree on the Ministry and Life of Priests* (n. 7) and the *Decree on the Pastoral Office of Bishops in the Church* (n. 28) and described in greater detail in the Motu Proprio *Ecclesiae*

---

bishop and priest; cf. B. Dupuy, "Is There a Dogmatic Distinction between the Function of Priests and the Function of Bishops?" in *Concilium* 34 (1968), pp. 74-86; A. W. J. Houtepen, "Het ambt in de structuur van de kerk," in *Vox Theologica* 37 (1967), pp. 269-291; F. Klostermann, "Pastoral-theologische Perspektive," in *Der Priester in einer säkularisierten Welt* (1968), pp. 88-106.

[12] Cf. O. Schreuder, "Die kirchliche Amtsstruktur in unserer Zeit," in *Der Priester . . . , op. cit.,* pp. 76-87.

Sanctae (n. 15), is an important move forward toward an integrated organization of pastoral work. If this council of priests is to be effective, it must of course fulfill certain conditions. Thus, if one wishes to maintain its advisory character, this should not be overemphasized, as it would only have a paralyzing effect. (Personally I do not think that it is dogmatically necessary to maintain it, and it seems even wrong if we want to do justice to the collegial element in Church government alongside of the personal element; the tensions which can hardly be avoided in this case are, from the evangelical point of view, preferable to an episcopal autocracy.) Then, this council must meet regularly with a well-prepared agenda concerned with really important pastoral matters, including matters of faith and morals.

And if we wish to take seriously the concept of the People of God and the evangelical view of ecclesiastical office as a service to this People, there must be close cooperation and an exchange of ideas between this council of priests and the diocesan pastoral council of which religious and lay people are also members. Better still, perhaps, is the idea introduced in the diocese of Breda where there is one pastoral council which embraces both.[13] For more specific questions concerning the executive aspect of practical pastoral work, the appropriate body would seem to be the diocesan pastoral center.

The Concrete Experience of Communal Responsibility.

The realization of collegiality at the top through collective discussion and direction does not yet guarantee a genuine integration of pastoral care. The discussion will lose relevance if it is not constantly fed from the grass roots. Directives agreed upon will remain purely theoretical unless they are actually put into practice through mutual cooperation. Only if these conditions are fulfilled will the priests experience their council as something that represents them genuinely to the bishops.[14] Here the situa-

---

[13] Cf. H. Verbeek, "Nieuwe structuren voor de R. K. kerk in Nederland," in *Vox Theologica* 37 (1967), pp. 292-320. A fair amount of information on this subject can be found in *Pastorale Gids* (Rotterdam).
[14] *Decree on the Ministry and Life of Priests,* n. 7.

tion should not be dominated by the idea of "participation" but rather by the awareness of a common responsibility for preaching the Gospel, celebrating the liturgy and pastoral guidance. The distinction between bishop and priest should not be seen so much in a difference of spiritual power as in the difference of the level and extent of its exercise. The same function which the priest fulfills for a limited group, at a specific place or in a special field, is fulfilled by the bishop for a larger group or a larger region. The distinction is therefore more quantitative than qualitative, although the former will imply the latter to a certain extent. This is connected with the New Testament where not only the local community is truly "the Church" but where this term also applies to regions or countries, and yet is used in the singular. The council of priests and the pastoral council constitute the collegial element at the diocesan level; the bishop represents the personal element in the guidance of the diocesan Church.[15]

The Limitations of the Presbyterium, the Basic Charismatic Structure of the Church and Variety of Functions

The view just mentioned facilitates the transition toward collegiality at the basic level. There, too, both the personal and the collegial elements must be recognized. The link between priests, created by their common functional charism, must find expression in a close cooperation at ground level. However, the rediscovery of the basic charismatic structure of the Church has had a twofold effect. The first is that the ecclesial office allows for and even demands a far greater differentiation and variation than that contained in the three offices of bishop, priest and deacon. The second is that the office can only function at its best when it gives rise to, recognizes and stimulates the free charism.[16] This is bound to result in a lessening of the distance between the officeholder and the layman which will make itself felt increasingly and lead to a fluid transition from one to the other. This

[15] Cf. *Rapport over het ambt*, ed. by Prof. Dr. H. Berkhof, and put before the General Synod of the Dutch Reformed Church in 1968.

[16] Cf. H. Küng, *op. cit.*, pp. 360f.; R. Bunnik, *Dienaren van het aggiornamento* (Nijmegen/Utrecht, 1967); O. Schreuder, *op. cit.*

widens the basis for an integration of pastoral work. The presbyterium has become too narrow a platform for this kind of operation, forming only a part of it, and that not even the most important part.

New Structures in Pastoral Work

The consequences of all this for the restructuring of pastoral work must be thought out more thoroughly and rediscovered partly by experiment. Advisory structures such as the deanery and parochial councils must be inserted. Here free discussion groups can play a real part as long as they are well managed and care is taken of the necessary feedback. Therefore, I would like to draw attention to some conditions which must be fulfilled at the clerical level if we really want to lead this restructuring toward pastoral integration.[17]

A *first condition* is a *certain homogeneous conception among the clergy about the content and extent of their function.* This holds particularly for the ideas about authority both among themselves (parish priest-curate, team leader-member) and in their relation toward the laity. If one appreciates lay initiatives and wishes to incorporate them, while the other sees the laity only as the object of pastoral care with no other function than to obey, there is *no possibility of any fruitful cooperation.* Second, the clergy must reach far-reaching agreement in their attitude toward the situation in Church and society. This demands that common study and constant discussion which may lead to a well-founded common attitude and a clear directive. Third, there must be a certain *readiness to accept change in function and status.* With all the social and cultural changes that are taking place in the world, the clergy must be prepared to accept a carefully thought out adjustment. This requires flexibility, self-criticism and the ability to accept the criticism of others and to use it for improvement in their work. It is equally necessary that they

[17] This information is taken from two investigations carried out by H. Labriaire and W. Rongen, students in pastoral theology at the University of Nijmegen.

positively query the autarchy of the parish and feel the need for both a wider cooperation and the integration of their own work into a wider context of ward, town or deanery. Only this integration alone can lead to a rational distribution of the available forces. Finally, room will have to be made for *differentiation within the actual fulfillment of the pastoral task*. The distribution of the work must be guided by the ability and preference of those concerned. This will help to leave space for a certain autonomy within the framework of close cooperation.

An investigation in two Dutch deaneries has shown that many priests are still unwilling to fulfill these conditions. They are quite willing to accept pastoral integration in theory and in the abstract, but in many cases the practical realization is obstructed by a mentality which is not ripe for it, although they are not conscious of this. New directives from the top, even if reached in collegial discussion at high level, remain a dead letter when they are not accompanied by a different, more rational handling of appointments and patient and expert guidance toward a change in the mentality.

Heinz Schuster/*Saarbrücken, West Germany*

Priestly Spirituality

W e can clearly grasp the difficulties confronting current theological reflection on priestly spirituality if we examine what Vatican Council II had to say in its *Decree on the Ministry and Life of Priests*. To begin with, we still find the underlying presupposition that there is a priestly *state* to which all priests belong, no matter what their individual duties may be (n. 8). Even leaving this aside, we encounter problems when we read the sections on the "priestly life" (nn. 12-14) and its "special spiritual needs" (nn. 15-17), for here we find concepts, theological categories, analogies and motivations that belong to the muddied and myth-shrouded theological waters of the past. Priests "take on the likeness of Christ" (n. 12). They have "a special obligation to acquire perfection" because they were "consecrated afresh to God when they were ordained" (n. 12). They have been made "living instruments of Christ" (n. 12), and Vatican Council II urges them "to use every means the Church recommends . . . to attain an ever greater personal holiness" so that they will become "more fitting instruments in the service of the whole People of God" (n. 12).

The Decree goes on to discuss priestly holiness, taking for granted that there is a distinctive brand of priestly holiness (n. 13). When it comes to the problem of reconciling the priest's many external activities with a vital interior life, the Decree simply points to the example of Christ "who accomplished his task by making the will of God his daily bread" (n. 14). This merely reiterates a past cliché, as if that were enough to tell us what God wills of his instruments here and now.

The Decree goes on to discuss the need to "work in communion with their brother priests". Put concretely: "Obedience and a spirit of faith leads them to accept and carry out the instructions and recommendations of the pope, the bishop and other superiors. However humble and lowly their task, they should accept it with the utmost willingness and spend themselves in discharging it" (n. 15).

There is not much room for talk about the necessity for collaboration with the other segments of the Christian community, because they are "the flock committed to their care" (n. 14). This old and basic misconception is repeated once again!

Nor is any room provided for the possibility of disagreeing with "those whom God has appointed visible rulers of his Church" (n. 15). Indeed, the Decree spells out the concrete way in which the priest can model himself after Christ: he must show "humility and obedience, responsible and gladly given, [to] those who are principally responsible for ruling the Church of God" (n. 15). A parallel is set up between Christ's obedience to the will of his Father (who is God, after all) and the priest's obedience to the will of his superiors (n. 15)!

Much Imprecision Evident

These conciliar statements on the work and "spiritual life" of the priest are symptomatic of the difficulties that must be faced by any theologian who tackles the question of priestly spirituality. Four major difficulties can be pinpointed:

1. In many such statements we find that the determining factor is "Jesus", "Christ the priest", or "God", but we do not find any well-grounded christology at all. Moreover, little note is taken of the fact that priestly spirituality, too, must operate within a world that changes from day to day.

2. When the question arises how priestly spirituality is to

work itself out concretely, the answer is usually the same. Specific pious exercises and a specific pattern of external conduct are laid down as the guiding norm for priestly spirituality. This easily gives rise to the misconception that priestly spirituality is something we can measure, learn and make comparisons about.

3. The distinctiveness and individuality of "priestly spirituality" over against Christian spirituality in general are presumed from the start. If any attempt is made to justify this differentiation, it is all too often based on differences in function within the Church, on differences in ecclesiastical office, or on differences in their state in life.

4. If the relationship between spirituality and the Christian ethos is pondered at all, the usual response is that spirituality is a special instance of the overall Christian ethos. The former is the ideal and acme of the latter. Time and again the assertion is made that true perfection can only be found where this special spirituality is sought after, but little proof is offered to back up this assertion.

The Nature of Christian Spirituality

Spirituality, in general, may be viewed as man's basic existential attitude and approach to life. It is the product and the expression of his religious or ethical outlook, of his own commitment as a person.[1] The distinctive nature of Christian spirituality, then, must be sought in the nature and purpose of Christian commitment.

This latter question is not given a full theological answer, however, by simply pointing to "Jesus", "Christ the priest" or "the will of God" as our goal. For one thing, Jesus does not simply represent some transcendent, other-worldly spirituality that we struggle vainly to reach from here with our frail human efforts. Jesus is the great historical happening within this world, in which we encounter God's definitive yes to humanity and to our world.[2]

[1] Cf. Hans Urs von Balthasar, "The Gospel as Norm and Test of All Spirituality in the Church," in *Concilium* 9 (1965), pp. 7-23.
[2] Cf. 2 Cor. 1, 19.

"Jesus Christ" means that human nature has a beginning and a future, ordained from all eternity by God and inseparable from him. Life, which we now hold on to by a thread, is not the brief beginning of something doomed to end; it is the God-given chance, the grace, that should mature into permanent union with God through our persistent free consent in the course of time. Thus, without doing injustice to the theological and christological aspects involved, we can say this: the authentic and ultimate basis of Christian spirituality is life, insofar as it is the embodiment of the grace that has been given to us, and its dimensions and future prospects are revealed to us in Jesus, the God-Man.

Thus Christian spirituality begins where this "given" humanity is grasped as a real opportunity, whose future lies beyond our own innate potential and capacity, and it finds fulfillment basically in hope-filled, courageous commitment to the human race and the world, which God so loved that he gave up his only begotten Son for their sake (Jn. 3, 16). There is no other "will of God" for us outside of his forgiving, merciful love for us and the world, a love which turns us into his children and thus sanctifies us. When we say that the Gospel is the norm and test of all Christian spirituality, we must spell out more clearly what that means. It means that the norm and test and ultimate orientation of all Christian spirituality is the future laid out for man by God in the Gospel,[3] where God and man become inseparable for all eternity without ever becoming intermingled.

The Spirit of Jesus Conditions All Christian Spirituality

The Gospel, as described above, represents an opportunity and an open-ended future for all men (1 Tim. 2, 4); it is a future opened up to man by God and already "at hand" in the world (cf. Mk. 1, 15). This being the case, all Christian spirituality must be viewed as a wondrous surprise, as a happening that we can never grasp adequately in rational terms and that is already

[3] Cf. J.-B. Metz, "Grundstrukturen im heutigen Verständnis der Kirche zur Welt," in *Handbuch der Pastoraltheologie* II/2 (Freiburg 1966) pp. 239-267, especially p. 246.

there before man's free will and commitment come into play. Before man takes cognizance of this happening, before he ponders and accepts it, God has already committed himself to man and called for a commitment from man. Before man can adequately formulate his own faith, hope and spirituality, God's fidelity and the Spirit of hope have already been given to him as an opportunity. "We do not know what we should pray for as we ought, but the Spirit himself pleads for us with unutterable groanings" (Rom. 8, 26).

The Spirit is "another advocate" (Jn. 14, 16) who has been given to us. He is the one Spirit of the one faith and the one hope in the one Father of all (Eph. 4, 6). He cannot be partitioned or manipulated, nor can he be intensified by a human training process or thereby differentiated. If Christian spirituality is, first and foremost, this wondrous happening in hope to which we are submitted (Rom. 8, 20), and commitment to this hope, which applies equally to all men and the whole of creation, then there can be only *one* Christian spirituality. Any further distinctions, based on "spiritual works", pious practices or good deeds, are necessarily secondary (1 Cor. 12, 11).

The Spirituality of the Gospel Servant

The dependence of this one Christian spirituality on the Spirit of Jesus has often been forgotten by Christianity in the past. Indeed, it is a standing temptation, because all spirituality tends to become embodied in concrete forms, and men tend to believe that these forms can be learned, regulated and mandated. Theologically speaking, man can never prove conclusively of which spirit he is the child, but he keeps on trying to do this, passing off his awkward efforts, his pious airs and certain pronouncements as those of the "Spirit".

All this gives us some standard for judging the past, and for taking heed in the future. All too often we have tied up the notion of "spiritual living" exclusively with the priesthood, even though there is no theological legitimacy for doing this. Genuine Christian spirituality and real spiritual life are not defined in terms of belonging to some particular state or office in the Church. Nor is it permissible to speak about a special or more perfect spirituality solely when it is a question of priestly spirituality.

We are justified in talking about a "special" spirituality only when we are talking about a group of Christians who have committed themselves to the Gospel in a more deliberate, intensive and clear-cut way—and here we use "Gospel" in the sense that it is the relevant comment about the meaning of human life and man's world. This "special" spirituality, then, would be the expression of a "special" commitment. In other words, insofar as there are Christians who deliberately and expressly see themselves as servants of God and his Gospel, there can be a specific and distinctive "Gospel-servant spirituality", and the free commitment of the individual Christian would be his obedient reaction to the human commitment called for by the Gospel.

Now this does not destroy the essential unity of Christian spirituality. It merely recognizes the fact that when human beings are involved, there can be different degrees of surprise, reflection and commitment. One would be hard put to prove that our distinction here represents a new attempt to formulate a special spirituality for some chosen or more perfect group.

Some Essential Features of This Servant Spirituality

The Gospel suggests quite a bit about the spirituality we have been discussing:

1. The servants of Jesus and his Gospel have been *called*; they have not made the choice on their own (Jn. 13, 18; 15, 16). Their task is a gift. Pride, vanity, class consciousness, esoterism and other such feelings are unjustified and illegitimate.

2. All these servants are given *exactly the same opportunity, exactly the same grandeur,* and *exactly the same reward* (Mt. 20, 1-16). There is no place for a "spiritual" hierarchy.

3. The servants of the Gospel have a strict and unconditional duty to be *merciful,* because mercy has been shown to them (Mt. 18, 23-35). They are not to measure, to judge or to condemn (Lk.

6, 37f.). The harvest is not their concern, and they are not to worry about the weeds (Mt. 13, 24-30).

4. Insofar as the servants of the Gospel have recognized and reflected upon their master's will, they will be punished and beaten for mistreating his other servants and carousing in his absence (Lk. 12, 45-48). Whoever beats another servant will be numbered among the unfaithful (Lk. 12, 46).

5. Unconditional efficiency and productivity are expected from the servants of the Gospel. Whatever is entrusted to them (and it is the Gospel!) is not to be buried in the ground for safekeeping. They are to allow it to bear fruit for God (Lk. 19, 12-27; see also Mt. 25, 14-30).

6. Despite this obligation to bear much fruit, the servants of the Gospel must regard themselves as useless and unprofitable (Lk. 17, 10). They are replaceable and not indispensable. They themselves owe their opportunity to the mercy which God has shown them. Their first and primary proclamation must be: "*I* was and still am an object of God's mercifulness"—not, "The *other* person needs God's mercy."

7. There is only *one* Father of all (Eph. 4, 6), *one* mankind loved by God, *one* world loved by God, and *one* Gospel for mankind in this world. But there are *different* ministries to this one Gospel. Insofar as they are appeals (charisms) of the one Spirit, they are all equally necessary and on a par with each other. They are not some societal or ecclesiastical office, nor are they under the rule of such an office. "Office" in the Church is rather a service to the Gospel in the unity of faith and in the recognition of the Son of God (cf. Eph. 4, 11ff.). If this office is exercised without the Spirit, without the influence of true Christian spirituality, it may still be an office in juridical or sociological terms, but it has ceased to be a service on behalf of the Gospel and the Church's true mission (Rom. 8, 9).

All the ministries in the Church have, in the last analysis, only *one* meaning and aim: to arouse faith in the Gospel among men of every time and place. Are the servants helping to realize the future that has been opened to mankind and his world in Jesus

Christ? Are they helping to keep alive man's God-given hope in the merciful and optimistic significance of life? In short, are they keeping alive the Spirit? The answers to these questions will decide the vitality and effectiveness of all Christian spirituality; they will serve as the measuring rod for the spirituality of the servants of the Gospel.

Perspectives

We have briefly sketched the references to Christian spirituality that are to be found in the Gospel. But we would simply repeat an old error of the past if we were to try to use them as the framework for a systematic and casuistic treatment of priestly spirituality. The spirituality of the Gospel servant is not just composed of abstract spiritual attitudes and reflections. It is constructive, fruitful behavior—hence, behavior in the world and in human society.

Nor can we regard the Gospel references as a catalogue of norms and laws, or Christian spirituality itself as simply the fulfillment of laws and norms to perfection. For one of the decisive features in general Christian spirituality, as well as in the "particular" spirituality of those who become special servants of the Gospel, is that they take history seriously, viewing it as part of the world for which God showed such great love.

However, we encounter history in the varied free decisions and actions of others, which cannot be predicted in advance, regulated or manipulated. They are part of the "now" situation in which we live. This situation cannot be accounted for in any list of norms or laws for spiritual living. We must explore them with an open, prudent, committed Christian spirit, analyze the challenge they pose, and react to them sympathetically in a Christian manner.

The specific spirituality of the servant of the Gospel, then, is embodied more in careful hearing than in obedient heeding. It does not turn a deaf ear to the present or move apart from its new structures, questions and challenges. The person who closes himself to the present is one who, in the last analysis, closes himself to the future—the future that we must bring to realization, the future that has lost all its overtones of terror because God is for us (Rom. 8, 31) and has provided a happy ending out of the tattered shreds of our history.

The spirit of hope does not live on the motto: Take no risks. Before us lies the ultimate promise of grace: God's ultimate and definitive communication of himself to us. If we cling to this promise but do not go out after it with courage, magnanimity and even rashness (cf. Lk. 16, 1-9), we may well be numbered among the pious and the saintly but we are in danger of extinguishing the Spirit.

Now we do not mean to suggest at all that skepticism, doubt, desperation and the long shadow of inescapable death (i.e., sadness) have no place in Christian spirituality. Not only theological precision but also human sincerity demands that we not erase the line which separates us from God, our handful of life from the whole of life, our humanity from the humanity willed and loved by God, our impotence from the power of his love for us. There is no genuine Christian spirituality that does not contain that impotent, desperate, yet obstinate conviction of hope that we shall win out, not because *we* are working at it but because *God* has guaranteed us victory.

Finally, at this point in our treatment, a word must be said about the "spirit of solidarity" and its importance for Christian spirituality. We are not concerned here with a theoretical or theological acknowledgment of the fact that humanity was envisioned and redeemed by God as a unified whole. We want to stress, rather, a new recognition and appreciation of each individual's tieup with the evangelical message of forbearance, mercifulness, and God's fidelity and loyalty to us. Again and again the Church's preaching office may be misconstrued as a mission to pass on divine information to man. But the spirit of the Gospel is only to be found where the servant of the Gospel conveys his own surprise and neediness in his proclamation, where he speaks as sinner to sinner, where he readily admits his own astonishment, lack of comprehension, lack of faith, and hesitations, where he confesses his own impotence and remains skeptical about his own knowledge and goodness.

We must not forget that Christian *perfection,* which all too often is plotted out as the goal of priestly spirituality, can never be attained by going into spiritual isolation; it is an aspect and a consequence of Christian brotherhood. The person who measures himself against others, concluding that he is better, higher, purer, holier, more pious, more knowledgeable and more faithful, has the perfection of the Pharisees.

No Christian is in a position to pass judgment on others, and hence to pass judgment on himself. Even "pastoral considerations" and "concern for the salvation of others" do not enable us to form such a judgment. The other person is never the measuring rod for our own "perfection". *He* is the task which has been set for us. God loves and looks out for *him,* God has chosen *him,* God waits for *him,* God has picked *him* out of the herd of ninety-nine good sheep. *He,* in his freedom, is incomparable and irreplaceable. *He* is the one to whom the Gospel, and hence our ministry, are directed.

We have no edge or advantage over him. We have no better or greater opportunity than he does. His opportunity is our opportunity as well. When we understand the Gospel correctly, the spirituality of Christian brotherhood is not so much an *imitation of Christ* as an *encounter with him;* he has become the brother of all mankind, and in our human brothers we truly encounter him.

Karl Rahner, S.J./*Münster, West Germany*

What Is the Theological Starting Point for a Definition of the Priestly Ministry?

The priestly ministry in the Catholic Church is an extremely complex factor and subject to the vicissitudes of history. In the concrete it is determined not only by the dogmatic essence of the Church herself and her own real theological nature, belonging as it does to the "divine right" of the Church, but also by the concrete historical condition of the Church and the consequent social and changing position of the priest within the ecclesial community and the recognition of his function by secular society. Here, however, I want to limit myself to the *theological* starting point for the definition of the nature of the priestly ministry in the Church. Everything else is left aside, however much it contributes to the present crisis in the priest's self-understanding and to other genuine theological issues.

The enduring theological nature of the priesthood is of course constantly influenced by other factors and causes of an historical and social kind which affect his concrete position, and to that extent these questions—here not methodically dealt with—constitute the background to our real question. But although the priestly ministry is in its theological essence a very complex factor, so that one should beware of deriving too "speculative" conclusions about its total reality from a radically simple characteristic, the present theory and practice of a priest's life show that

we *have to ask* what the initial *starting point* is from which we
can reach a definition of its theological nature, because only then
can we see clearly which elements belong to its enduring nature
and which to changing historical conditions and circumstances.[1]

I

NEGATIVE PRELIMINARY REMARKS

The present concrete situation of the priest and theological
argument show already that it is not very helpful to determine
the nature of the priesthood right from the start by those *sacramental powers* with which, according to conciliar teaching (especially the Council of Trent), the priest is endowed and which
thus distinguish him from the laity and the lower ranks of the
hierarchical office (particularly the deacon)—in other words,
the power to administer the eucharist and sacramental confession
(together with the anointing of the sick). To see here that the
first and basic starting point for the self-understanding of a priest
is no longer adequate needs no elaboration. Moreover, such a

[1] One cannot document every single thought in a short article. I refer
therefore to other basic studies where I have dealt with this subject:
Kirche und Sakramente (Freiburg, ² 1963), pp. 85-95; "Die Träger des
Selbstvollzugs der Kirche," in *Handbuch der Pastoraltheologie* I, ed. by
F. X. Arnold, K. Rahner, V. Schurr, L. M. Weber (Freiburg, 1964), pp.
149-215, esp. pp. 154f.; "Amt und Charisma," *ibid.*, pp. 179f.; "Presbyterium und der einzelne Priester" (Freiburg, 1969); *Vom Sinn des
kirchlichen Amtes* (Freiburg, 1966); *Knechte Christi* (Freiburg, 1967);
"Priesterliche Existenz," in *Schriften zur Theologie* III (Einsiedeln,
⁶ 1964), pp. 285-312; "Der eine Mittler und die Vielfalt der Vermitt-
lungen," in *Schr. zur Theol.* VIII (Einsiedeln, 1967), pp. 218-35. Two
more recent studies are being printed: *Theologische Ueberlegungen zum
Priesterbild von heute und morgen* (Veröff. der Kath. Akademie in
Bayern, Munich) and *Das Dild des Priesters heute* (Address given at the
Priestertag des Deutschen Katholikentages in Essen, Sept. 1968, to be
published by the Bonifacius-Verlag, Paderborn). For the idea of "office",
see my commentary on Chapter 3 of the *Constitution on the Church* in
Das II. Vatikanische Konzil. Konstitutionen, Dekrete und Erläuterungen.
(Freiburg, 1966), pp. 210-46. For n. 28, see the commentary given by
P. A. Grillmeier on pp. 247-55.

starting point has no immediately intelligible foundation in the Bible.

Nor is it helpful to see this starting point in the *concept of the* "mediator". This concept, too, is not directly covered by the Bible, since Scripture applies the concept of mediator only to Jesus Christ. Moreover, such a starting point immediately implies difficulties such as how precisely the priestly ministry participates in Christ's mediatorship, how this participation is related to other functions of mediation which exist in the body of Christ outside the priesthood, and how exactly we must understand such a mediatorship, since this mediation can only serve the already immediate relationship between God and the human person-in-grace. Such a starting point would also have to explain the dogmatic fact that all sacramental mediation is but a particular, though effective, manifestation of a grace-filled relationship between God and man, a relationship which operates in human life in all its dimensions also without such a mediation by priestly ministry.

II
POSITIVE PRESUPPOSITIONS

The Oneness and Divisibility of "Office" in the Church

From the point of view of the Bible, the history of dogma and theology, it is a fact that if we want to understand the theological nature of the priestly ministry (as distinct from episcopacy, diaconate and laity), we cannot begin by taking for granted the three degrees of the hierarchical office in the Church and its distinction from the rest of the "People of God". We should rather start (although this cannot be done here) from the nature of the Church as the sacrament of God's gift of himself to the world in faith, hope and charity. From here we should then go on to show, with constant reference to Scripture, that the Church thus understood is always in need of what one can call an "office", the nature of which is determined on the one hand by the nature of the Church herself and on the other by certain negative limitations, since it is one particular function in the Church among others through which the Church fulfills herself.

This "office", then, is primarily one as the Church herself is originally one. This *one* "office" must be broken up into particular functions both because of the officeholders and because of the tasks and powers which its nature demands. Without such a distribution the nature of the Church as a social reality would be unthinkable. Such a distribution, however, can take place in very different ways, even if it is taken for granted that the development of this distribution into three degrees during the apostolic age is fixed and permanently binding for the post-apostolic Church, and in this sense "of divine right". For in the New Testament itself this distribution of the *one* office is still very fluid, and the exact content of these three degrees (taken for granted here, for argument's sake) remains wide open in the New Testament and beyond.

These three degrees do not necessarily and dogmatically imply that, within or alongside of these three, there can be no other functions which are themselves also genuine, though historically conditioned, diversifications of the *one* office. This is clear from history where we see that within and alongside of the three accepted functions there are very different functions carried out by other officeholders. This holds also for the sacramental transmission of such a function to a particular officeholder. There is no dogma which says that only the conferring of episcopacy, "priestly ministry" and diaconate is a sacrament. This would at least be in contradiction with medieval theology.

Without discussing whether it is opportune, it is therefore quite thinkable theologically that, even within the theory of the three degrees, the functions contained in the *one* office of the Church can be distributed and sacramentally conferred in a different manner, so that, for instance, the concept "priesthood" can cover varying and sacramentally conferred functions or that there can be other sacramentally conferred "leading" functions (from the ecclesial point of view) apart from the priesthood, such as the office of "teacher" or "community leader". According to tradition and in current terminology such a function is only called "priestly" when it includes administering the eucharist and the other sacramental powers already mentioned. But even this does not take away the fact that in principle the Church has a great deal of liberty to distribute her *one* office according to the demands of the situation and the functions which flow from her nature within this *one* office.

The Operative Character of the Word in the Church

In our search for a simple, biblical and practicable starting point for a definition of the nature of the priestly office, we cannot forget that the Word, entrusted to the Church, is in principle something which makes things happen, which manifests and is operative, and not merely the communication of something that is unconnected with the communication of doctrine. The Church fulfills her own being as the sacrament of God's gift of himself to the world in the Word, and this Word has therefore basically a "manifesting" character. What this Word proclaims happens. This "eventful" character of the Word has, like the ordinary human word, essentially various levels. And so it reaches its highest level in what we call, in the technical-theological sense of the word, the sacrament, but this essential difference of level in its operative character, this "effectiveness" of the Word, does not invalidate this basic character of every ecclesial word as the anamnetic or prognostic re-presentation of an "event" of salvation. The proclaiming of the Word and the administering of the sacraments have therefore a common root and are ultimately one in nature.[2]

---

[2] For further development, see "Wort und Eucharistie," in *Schr. zur Theol.* IV (Einsiedeln, [5] 1967), pp. 313-35; "Zur Theologie des Symbols," in *Schr. zur Theol.* IV. pp. 275-311; "Die Gegenwart des Herrn in der christlichen Kultgemeinde," in *Schr. zur Theol.* VIII (Einsiedeln, 1967), pp. 395-408. The arguments given in the essays here referred to will prevent the statements made in this article from being misunderstood.

III
THE STARTING POINT ITSELF

Attempt at a Definition

Having made these various observations we may say, perhaps somewhat riskily because briefly, that *the priest is he who, related to an at least potential community, preaches the Word of God by mandate of the Church as a whole and therefore officially, and in such a way that he is entrusted with the highest levels of sacramental intensity of this Word.* Expressed very simply, he has the mission to preach the Gospel in the name of the Church. He does this at the highest level at which this Word can operate in the anamnesis of Christ's death and resurrection through the celebration of the eucharist.

In this definition we are not concerned with the distinction between priesthood and episcopacy. That this distinction should not be underrated is clear from the fact that medieval theology attached a sacramental character to the consecration of a bishop, even though this can no longer be maintained in this way since Vatican Council II. This definition shows that the priest is not simply a "cult official" and that this witnessing to the Word in its manifest concrete saving capacity involves his whole existence (seen theologically), regardless of how far it may determine his life in terms of a secular profession or support him economically. As the foundation of his priesthood the proclamation of God's Word gives this priesthood a *missionary* character from the start and relates it to a community, regardless of whether he can already presuppose it or must still create it, and also regardless of the sociological composition of this community. Having said this, we do not exclude that there are or may be wholly different ways of "serving the Word" which are "official" and can be bestowed on anyone by sacramental conferment.

What Can, and What Cannot,
Change in the Catholic Priesthood?

From what has been said it should be clear that the *concrete form* of such a priestly commission is open to all kinds of variations from the point of view of ecclesiastical or secular sociology, and that in fact many functions undertaken by a given priest can be thought of as proper, non-priestly, functions in the Church without affecting the theological nature of the priesthood itself. There can be great differences in the manner of proclamation, in the actual condition of the community to which the priest is related, in the more careful coordination of various existing or possible offices in the Church and in the priest's status in secular society.

All this must not be identified *a priori* with the priest's proper theological nature. Moreover, all this is not simply subject to factual changes but should be constantly and actively reviewed by the Church. Up till now too little attention has been paid to this possibility of internal and external changes in the Church's office in general and in the priestly office in particular, often by appealing to the "indelible character" of the priesthood. But today exegesis, the history of dogma, the history of the Church, ecclesiastical sociology and the needs of the contemporary Church force us to take a more radical look at what can and what cannot change in the Catholic priesthood. If we pursue this line of thought courageously we shall see that there is, on the one hand, an enduring element in the priestly office which justifies a modern man's undertaking this office courageously and confidently, while on the other hand the Church has from the point of view of dogma an almost unlimited freedom to shape and distribute her office in such a way that it really corresponds to her mission and the present situation.

Stefan Barela/*Czestochowa, Poland*

Vita Communis: Contacts, Communities and Communitary Forms of Secular Priests

The title of this article contains three complementary notions designated by the words "contacts", "communities" and "communitary forms". Contacts of priests express a certain community, or a tendency toward the formation of a community, with a stable character of existence and action. Hence, we can consider community as a fundamental notion.

I

FUNDAMENTAL NOTIONS

Contacts of priests, considered from the viewpoint of relations of daily life and under the aspect of action and even pastoral collaboration, have a transitory character. If they are not completely fortuitous, but connected with the realization of well-defined priestly and pastoral tasks, they then constitute a step toward the formation of a community characterized by a certain stability. We can attribute to such a community stable, distinctive traits from the ontological, moral and psychological viewpoint. We might say that contacts so conceived are to communities what actions are to moral or intellectual capabilities.

A more detailed analysis of the notion and the vital value of the community will provide the basis for an accurate understanding of the profundity of and the opportunity for contacts. Hence, starting from such an analysis, we could more accurately grasp the communitary forms of priests. The specific nature of these forms is conditioned not merely by reasons stemming from a definite purpose, life and action, but also by the external circumstances in which it must pursue those ends and accomplish concrete tasks.

The notion contained in the expression "vita communis" of secular priests can be conceived and interpreted in the proper and exact sense in stricter relation with the theology of the priesthood and above all with the mission of the priest. This notion comprises two elements in its traditional signification: the material element and the spatial element. The material element is constituted by a common dwelling and community table as well as by the community of other means necessary for the existence and life of the community.

The purpose of the community constitutes its spiritual element. The purpose is thus the formal factor of each community. The other elements are necessary in the measure that they effectively aid the attainment of the proposed purpose. This is why in all those communities of priests that have arisen in the Church, beginning with the apostolic college formed by Christ himself, the accent was placed on their supernatural purpose resulting from ordination and the priestly mission. A more profound conception of this purpose was connected with the process of evolution of the concept of community—from a juridical concept toward a theological and pastoral one.

II

BRIEF HISTORICAL SUMMARY OF THE PROBLEM

In an historical consideration of the process of formation of priestly communities, we can discern two currents: on the one hand, the initiatives of the Holy See and the bishops, and, on the other, the desires of numerous priests tending to assure themselves of stable conditions for the more holy and efficacious fulfillment of their priestly mission.

The prototype of all priestly communities is the apostolic college. Its spirit has been transmitted to the primitive groups of Christians who formed one perfect community. Its essence was expressed in the phrase "one heart and one soul" (Acts 4, 32).

The successive stages of the communitary movement of priests —beginning with the Synod of Toledo, through St. Gregory of Tours, and up to the Code of Canon Law—are characterized by the priority of the juridical element with respect to the theological element. In spite of this fact, we find in these institutions a certain dynamism of character in the search for a genre of community capable of responding to the needs of secular priests. After the Council of Trent St. Charles Borromeo (d. 1584) was the trailblazer in the work of creating priestly communities. In his episcopal household he created a veritable community of priests, living according to a Christian rule and performing the exercises of the spiritual life in common.

This community spirit imbued a good many secular priests, among whom we might cite St. Philip Neri, founder of the Roman Oratory (1577), M. Olier, M. Levêque, first superior of the community of St. Clement of Nantes, St. Louis-Marie Grignon de Montfort, and Cardinal Bérulle, founder of the French Oratory (1611).[1]

A major effort in the search for new forms specifically for the diocesan clergy was achieved by Barthélemy Holzhauser (1613-1658) who laid the foundation for an institution of priests in the diocese of Salzburg. His idea was also accepted in Poland, Italy, Sicily, Spain and France. The decisive point for the structural framework of this community was its complete dependence on

---

[1] M. Viller, "Communautaire (vie) dans le clergé diocésain," in *Dictionnaire de spiritualité* 11 (Paris, 1948), pp. 1161-63. Cf. J. Loew, *Comme s'il voyait l'invisible* (Paris, 1964); J. Hangouet, "Améliorer les communications dans la communauté," in *La vie spirituelle* 84 (1968), pp. 71-82; J. Daniélou, "Bien commun et bien des personnes," in *La vie spirituelle* 84 (1968), pp. 44-60.

the ordinary, without any exception. The originality of Holz-hauer's method lay in the fact that he did not express his idea in an artificial construction but based himself on the foundations of the Gospel and the living tradition of the Church.[2]

The Holy See looked favorably on the formation of communities-for-living of secular priests and granted them approval. Among the recent declarations of the popes we must mention *Exhortatio ad clerum* (August 4, 1908) in which St. Pius X expressed his joy at the fact that the time had arrived when the Church could see her priests deciding on a life in common.[3] The Code of Canon Law encourages even priests to create communities (Can. 134).

In Belgium Cardinal Mercier created the Brotherhood of the Friends of Jesus in 1918; in Italy parochial communities arose—for example, in Brescia, Navarre, Cuneo and Pompei. In Poland, in the diocese of Poznan, the "Societas Christi" was formed in 1934.[4]

This skimpy and very fragmentary historical summary of the problem gives evidence of an intrinsic process of the ever more profound awareness in the Church that the community of priests constitutes an indispensable value for the perfect accomplishment of the priestly mission. To verify this thesis, contemporary authors rightly appeal to the sources of revelation—in this case to tradition. Worthy of particular attention is the return to the idea of St. Ignatius of Antioch concerning the presbyterium of priests remaining in close union with one another and with their bishop. The latest theological works emphasize this unity under the aspect of the apostolic functions, defining the essence of the priesthood as a subordinated participation in the apostolic functions of the bishop. The diocesan union of priests with their bishop, united with the Holy Father, affects the union with the universal Church.[5]

[2] M. Viller, *ibid.*, pp. 1163-65.
[3] M. Viller, *ibid.*, p. 1167.
[4] M. Viller, *ibid.*, p. 1169.
[5] A. de Bovis, "Le presbytérat, sa nature et sa mission d'après le Concile du Vatican II," in *Nouvelle revue théologique* 89 (1967), pp. 1009-1042.

III
THE THEOLOGICAL CONCEPT OF THE COMMUNITY

Vatican Council II has accepted the term "presbyterium", enriching its content with profound theological data. It utilized this notion in the *Dogmatic Constitution on the Church,* affirming: "Priests, prudent cooperators with the episcopal order, its aid and instrument, called to serve the People of God, constitute one priesthood ['presbyterium'] with their bishop although bound by a diversity of duties." [6]

These functions indicate diverse sectors and spheres of the priestly ministry which the Council does not separate from the life of priests, holding them up as integral elements of the priestly mission. By the notion of "priestly mission" the Council means the *whole of the priestly vocation,* both as regards life and action —that is, the ministry. It establishes this notably by declaring: "Therefore, no priest is sufficiently equipped to carry out his own mission alone and, as it were, single-handedly. He can only do so by joining forces with other priests, under the leadership of those who are the rulers of the Church." [7] The theological foundations for priestly communities lead us to accept such a concept, for "all priests who are constituted in the order of priesthood by the sacrament of orders are bound together by an intimate sacramental brotherhood, but in a special way they form one priestly body in the diocese to which they are attached under their own bishop".[8]

This sacred character of priestly union stipulates a mission common to all priests: collaboration in the unique work of the "building up of the body of Christ". Priests have the responsibility for this task, and they cooperate in it, especially when they unite with their confreres through the bond of charity, prayer, and any kind of collaboration. Thus is manifested the unity de-

---

[6] *Dogmatic Constitution on the Church,* n. 28.
[7] *Decree on the Ministry and Life of Priests,* n. 7.
[8] *Ibid.,* n. 8.

sired by Christ, which will proclaim to the world that the "Son has been sent by the Father".[9]

Hence, the Council gives us a theological concept for the community of priests by accentuating its formal element—pastoral charity—for it is this that it asks of priests: "They . . . should always work within the bond of union with the bishops and their other fellow priests." [10]

IV

CONTACTS, COMMUNITIES AND COMMUNITARY FORMS OF SECULAR PRIESTS

Vatican Council II not only speaks of the general principles of priestly communities, but it also indicates the necessity of bringing about, or tending toward, their continual perfecting through "at least meeting at frequent intervals".[11] The personal and above all spiritual needs of priests necessitate the help and communion of other priests. So does the need for a prudent and harmonious pastoral action. Pastoral programs drawn up by episcopal conferences for an entire country demand a common commitment on the part of priests. Their success depends on a careful study of these programs which is accomplished through courses and regional conferences for priests. The purpose of the courses is the examination of theological principles of pastoral action, while the regional conferences also must be concerned with practical problems since they are oriented toward pastoral action as such.

The necessity to take into account all the pastoral needs of a particular environment makes it imperative to organize meetings of priests on the deanery or interdeanery level. This is especially true if the conditions and specific needs of particular regions of the diocese are to be considered. In addition, almost every parish has a specific character which requires local pastors to make an individual or collective effort to adapt the prevailing program to

9 *Ibid.*, n. 8.
10 *Ibid.*, n. 14.
11 *Ibid.*, n. 8.

their particular environment. In this sense, we can speak of contacts that are parochial, interparochial or deaneral, diocesan, interdiocesan, or nationwide.

Parochial Contacts

The contemporary concept of a parish requires that priests form a community in the strictest sense of the term. Living in common and sharing a common table are great goods, if they can be attained, but the contacts which refer to the basic duties of pastors come through as indispensable: the realization of definite pastoral programs and the responsibility for certain pastoral sectors or regions, such as regional catechetical groups, or centers of pastoral action, if possible, with pastors working in the same parish. The exchange of ideas and experiences, the desire to receive prudent advice, information concerning the life and work of priests—all these constitute frequent occasions for creating a parochial priestly community.

Interparochial-Deanery Contacts

Interparochial meetings of priests are related to concrete needs and pastoral tasks. They take place with profit both for the interior life of the priest and for the efficacy of his ministry. The priest's weekly confession and his spiritual conversations with his spiritual director, who is more often than not the spiritual father of the deanery, serve these needs to a certain extent. Monthly deanery conferences and days of recollection also provide for the spiritual needs of priests. The forms of professional and specialized pastoral work (for deaf-mutes and the blind, for example) in the process of formation create new planes of contacts among priests. Reciprocal services of priests specializing in certain sectors of pastoral work—within the limits of the deanery or on the interdeanery level—constitute other occasions for fruitful contacts.

All these contacts contribute to stimulate zeal and deepen pastoral charity. They express themselves practically in days of recollection organized for particular groups, according to profession, state of life, etc. and directed by priests of the deanery limits. Meetings of priest-catechists from certain regions of the diocese not only offer the possibility of perfecting methods of instructing in the faith but also deepen personal interior life. Systematic meetings of priest-officials of certain sectors of pastoral action in diverse regions of the diocese also contribute to the deepening of the interparochial community of priests.

Traditional get-togethers by reason of reciprocal pastoral services on the occasion of parish solemnities are in the process of progressive transformation into a community comprising the spiritual needs of the entire deanery. The role of the dean as organizer of pastoral action on the interdiocesan level is incontestably being enlarged. The postulate for organizing a deanery library to provide sustenance for the intellectual and spiritual life as well as the pastoral action of priests is brought forward more and more frequently. Certain houses for priests' retreats also tend toward community, especially those which cultivate prayer in common with young priests and foster the spirit of a fraternal priestly good will.

We must also make separate mention of contacts of priests with their bishop as he accomplishes his pastoral duties in the region—either on the occasion of a canonical visit, or by reason of his tour of larger parishes to administer the sacrament of confirmation or to take part in parish solemnities.

Diocesan and Interdiocesan Contacts

The contacts practiced until the present time by the diocesan clergy take on a theological motivation, a depth and a dynamic character, thanks to Vatican Council II which has indicated new aspects of the existing relations between priests and bishops. "All priests," says the Council, "share with the bishops the one identical priesthood and ministry of Christ." [12] In such a concept diocesan contacts express the pastoral charity of priests, for the love of the mystical body of Christ is realized in the diocese as part of the universal Church. The result is that contacts of priests, by their union with the bishop—the principle of diocesan unity—deepen the dispositions and possibly even the capability of the priest to cooperate in "building up the body of Christ".

[12] *Ibid.*, n. 7.

In Poland, the forms of common life for priests have inherited the ideas of St. Charles Borromeo, but the principles of Holzhauser which found approbation in the ranks of the clergy of Poland, especially in the dioceses of Wloclawek, Poznan and Lublin, played a decisive role in the formation of their spiritual physiognomy. The diocesan character was the most particular trait of these communities: in each diocese they adapted their forces to the actual conditions and needs.[13]

In the period between the two world wars the idea of a life in common was especially cultivated and consolidated by the Apostolic Union of the Priests of the Sacred Heart of Jesus. By means of a solid interior life, founded on the theological principles of the cult of the Sacred Heart of Jesus, it tended toward the effective formation of the attitude of social charity and the spirit of lasting community. An annual retreat of seven days and monthly or tri-monthly days of recollection aided the attainment of this end as well as favorable conditions—life in common in the full meaning of the word.

Retreats in common on the part of priests help deepen and perfect the sense of "co-responsibility" for the whole diocese. They also provide the occasion to create the atmosphere for a priestly community of prayer, which is a supernatural reflection of fraternal charity. Conferences and congregations of deans offer a good many opportunities for the formation of diocesan communities, for the deans—by their attitude and daily influence on priests in their region—can contribute effectively to the strengthening of the ties between priests and their deanery.

We must also mention the pastoral functions of the pastoral departments of diocesan chanceries which program, inspire and sustain priests in their pastoral activity. The pastoral departments carry out the programs of general or specialized pastoral work. On the national level, the particular sections of pastoral activity are directed by episcopal commissions.[14] Each of these commis-

---

[13] S. Dutkiewicz, "Lacznosc wsrod duchowienstwa," in *Miesiecznik koscielny* 7 (1911), pp. 92-96.

[14] Episcopal Commissions of Pastoral Work in Poland: Pastoral Commission, Marian Commission, Commission of Pastoral for Pastors, Commission of the Apostolate of the Laity, Commission of Conjugal Life and

sions has its counterpart in the diocesan departments of pastoral work. All the efforts of each group of persons responsible for diverse sectors of pastoral action in the diocese as well as the services of departments of pastoral work possess the character of close collaboration with those priests who concern themselves especially with action in the particular sector. These contacts often transform themselves into certain forms of community, by placing the accent on the priestly ministry and on collaboration.

Interdiocesan and National Contacts

The necessity for perspective in programming and the need to discuss and come to an agreement on the actual pastoral tasks necessitate more frequent contacts between the particular members of episcopal commissions mentioned above. These also number priests who are not bishops, in consideration of some specialization in the respective sectors of pastoral work. Contacts of diocesan departments and meetings on a national or interdiocesan level have the character of a certain continuity on the sphere of exchange of experiences and auxiliary materials for pastoral work.

The annual meetings of clergy in courses organized by the Catholic University of Lublin represent a form of engaging contacts for all. The actuality of problems and the interest brought to bear on the conciliar renewal create a favorable climate for the exchange of ideas. There is still another very special form of contacts on the national level: these are the meetings of priests on the occasion of pilgrimages to the national Marian Sanctuary of Czestochowa. There are groups which have for years been continuing a programmed pastoral action. We number under this heading especially pilgrimages or prayer days of professional or specialized pastoral work. Such contacts regularly take place among pastors of students, of those employed by the medical service, of women and young girls, of teachers, men and young boys, as well as pastors of deaf-mutes and the blind.

---

the Family, Commission of Pastoral for Women, Catechetical Commission, Commission of Pastoral for Students, Commission for Vocations, Commission for Films, Radio and Television.

The purpose and the program for these prayer days, which include participants from the whole country, constitute the object of considerations and preparations on the part of diocesan pastors throughout the country. The meeting of these priests immediately after the realization of the program of the prayer day contributes effectively to the deepening of pastoral formation. Here, the whole course of the day is discussed, a balance sheet of positive and negative things is drawn up, and conclusions for the future are reached.

We can add in the nature of an explanation that the Sanctuary of Czestochowa is the place for other more or less regular meetings of priests, during Mariological Congresses, Marian Days, days of recollection for pastors of sanctuaries of our Lady, and also for discussions on a national scientific level of the diverse disciplines of theology.

V

CONCLUSION

As is evident from these reflections, the present communities of priests, especially in Poland, have more of a theologico-pastoral character than a juridical one. The only remnants of the traditional communities are a few traits and tendencies of priestly spirituality. The vision and mission of the Church of Christ as revealed to us by Vatican Council II entail a theological deepening and a more dynamic conception of the community of priests. The Council connects the idea of the community of priests with the hope of perfect fulfillment of the mission assigned them by God and the Church.

Communities thus conceived will express in effective fashion the spirit of Vatican Council II and the adequate means of the conciliar renewal of the Church. The theological foundations for their activity and their apostolico-pastoral efficacy will doubtless be deepened in the process of the further development of the theology of the collegiality of bishops and of the mission of priests which is connected with it.

Norbert Greinacher/*Münster, West Germany*

The Non-Territorial Pastorate and the Part-Time Priest

I

THE TERRITORIAL AND NON-TERRITORIAL PASTORATE

We seem to have become thoroughly accustomed to a pastorate based on the geographically delimited parish. This structure is now generally considered to be normative, and any departure from it is seen as an emergency measure—and certainly as an abnormal one—that thereby confirms the territorial norm. The almost exclusive appeal of a territorially conceived pastoral structure made excellent sense in a stable society based on an agricultural economy, a society in which just about every aspect of community life (family, job, education, leisure, religious life, etc.) centered upon the unbroken confines of a village or—to use a modern expression—small town milieu.[1]

The Significance of the Functional Community

There are relatively few people who live in such a situation now. This means that in considering modern pastoral practice we must pay more attention than we have in the past to the existence in our society of other important groupings that are not defined by territorial boundaries but by other functions of social and

[1] Cf. Norbert Greinacher, *Die Kirche in der städtischen Gesellschaft* (Mainz, 1966), particularly pp. 358-62; *idem*, "Die funktionale Gemeinde," in *Handbuch der Pastoraltheologie* III (Freiburg, 1968), pp. 263-68.

community life: work, leisure, education, and so on. Because these are so important in themselves, we must not underestimate the significance of the non-territorial pastorate or the functional communities in which it operates. We must break away from the notion that territorially delimited pastoral work is the only one imaginable, without, however, going so far as to maintain that such a parish structure has no further role to play—for it has. Neither is it a question of rank: territorial parish first; ministering to the varying interest and work groups, second. The Church is realized in both forms of pastorate and in both forms of community.[2] Though that is certainly true in theory, in practice one often has the impression that those who gather together with workaday interests in common bring a greater degree of commitment to pastoral objectives than does the average parish community.

Functional Communities in Past Ecclesiastical Practice

A pastoral ministry geared to common interest groups is not a new phenomenon in the Church. Quite apart from brotherhoods like the medieval guilds, the Code of Canon Law expressly provides for such a pastorate.[3] For instance, Canon 216 refers to communities based upon language or nationality and made up of people who live in a particular town or district. Here the basic criterion of community membership is not habitat but language or nationality. Furthermore, the same Canon allows for the establishment of a parish based on local family groups or on workers at their place of work—though these are regarded as exceptions to the general rule. Examples of this sort of parish would be royal households, other sizable domestic establishments, prison or hospital staffs, military chaplaincies, and so on. In this connection I should also mention religious communities.

There are also functional communities which from the point of view of Canon Law do not have parish status. Such, for in-

---

[2] Cf. Karl Rahner, "Zur Theologie der Pfarre," in *Die Pfarre*, ed. Hugo Rahner (Freiburg, 1956), pp. 27-39.

[3] Cf. Eichmann and Mörsdorf, *Lehrbuch des Kirchenrechts* I (Paderborn, [8] 1963), pp. 340-42.

stance, are universities. Canon Law makes no provision for them, yet they necessarily represent a particular type of community assembled for a particular purpose. In this case pastoral practice has pursued solutions that, while not contrary to Canon Law, transcend its predominantly territorial emphasis.

If this can be achieved in the case of universities, it can also be achieved in other cases, and here and there it already has been. One thinks, for instance, of family groups, factory missions of various kinds, missions to the deaf and the blind, tourists centers, and so on. About such communities Karl Rahner has written: "Man as a social being belongs to his local neighborhood, to his particular professional grouping, to his particular cultural level, to his particular national group (which need not in all circumstances necessarily coincide with a given territory), to associations freely entered into, to groups formed according to age and sex, to groups formed by a common experience. All these social relationships and many others can have their importance as providing an occasion for the formation of groups to which the Church's message and teaching mission can be explicitly addressed, which can, according to circumstances, be the foundation of 'communities' in the theological sense, and which can also be the immediate context for the exercise of the individual Christian's apostolic responsibility." [4]

Role and Structure of the Functional Community

Given the sort of society we have today, it would be madness to insist upon an exclusive maintenance of a territorially delimited parish structure, for to do so would seriously hinder the preaching of the Gospel. Neither is it absolutely necessary that a pastorate based on shared interests be canonically enshrined. There is no reason at all why this type of community should not emerge from a particular situation that clearly requires it—for example, a large building site or a holiday resort—only to be dissolved as soon as the need has been met (the building is com-

[4] Karl Rahner, *Mission and Grace* III (London and New York, 1966), p. 60.

pleted, the holiday season ends). This sort of thing is already happening. There is always a danger in thinking in overformal terms: we must leave room for autonomy and elasticity. That said, it remains of the utmost importance that communities of this type are integrated as closely as possible into the Church as a whole; otherwise we simply run the risk of creating sects. In the integration process an important mediating role could be played by those new structures now emerging between the larger and more formal entities of deanery and diocese.[5]

II

THE PRESENT DEPLOYMENT OF PRIESTS

Unfortunately I do not have enough data to show how the present clerical strength is divided between the territorial and the non-territorial pastorate. Sufficient data does not exist. I can, however, say something about the German situation. For example, in 1959 there were 21,233 diocesan priests in East and West Germany together (including Berlin).[6] Of that number 2,673 (12%) were either retired or had been granted leave of absence. In the same year there were 7,060 religious, of whom 2,045 (29%) were primarily occupied in diocesan activities or in education. Breaking these figures down further, we have this picture: parish duties, 79% (84% seculars; 40% religious); schools, 9% (6% seculars; 34% religious); administration and sodalities, diocesan institutes and military chaplaincies, 12% (of whom 10% were seculars). In 1966 in the diocese of Essen 75% of the clergy worked in parishes, 15% in schools and just

—————
[5] Cf. Norbert Greinacher, "Der Vollzug der Kirche in der Diözese," in *Handbuch der Pastoraltheologie* III (Freiburg, 1968), pp. 59-110; *idem*, "Die Integration der Gemeinde in der Gesamtkirche," in *Die Neue Gemeinde*, ed. A. Exeler (Mainz, 1967), pp. 47-63.
[6] These and subsequent details concerning secular priests come from *Kirchliches Handbuch* XXV (Cologne, 1962), pp. 662f.; those concerning religious come from J. Dellepoort *et al.*, *Die deutsche Priesterfrage* (Mainz, 1961), p. 76.

under 10% were primarily employed in other pastoral work or in administration.[7]

These few details I offer only as specimen data. Clearly a more thorough piece of research would show a much more differentiated picture. Nevertheless, the basic outline would not greatly change.

III

AN ASSESSMENT OF THE SITUATION

If somebody asks whether priests are employed where they are most needed, or whether they are employed with a view to optimal efficiency, it must first of all be observed that they are now in such short supply that even to effect a moderately satisfactory deployment of personnel is extraordinarily difficult. In every area of pastoral activity there is a manpower deficiency. On the other hand it is precisely in circumstances of this sort that very carefully planned research—based on what we have, what we need, where we need it most and what we may expect—is indispensable. It does often seem that those concerned are still unaware of this. All too often a process of makeshift gap-plugging is to be observed in a situation that requires long-term strategic planning.

For example, given the present situation, one must ask in all seriousness whether there is sufficient justification for the employment in Germany of almost 2,000 priests in schools (the French figure for 1956, according to F. Boulard's estimate, was 5,300).[8] I am well aware how difficult it is to solve problems of this sort and yet to me it does seem wrong that such a large proportion of total manpower should be used in this way (many of these priests are even teaching secular subjects) when there is sure dire need for their services in other fields. It is at least

[7] See Report 44 of the Sozialinstitut des Bistums Essen—*Kirchliche Sozialforschung* (Essen, 1967).

[8] *Die europaische Priesterfrage* (Vienna, 1959), p. 97.

difficult to maintain that the pastoral potential of these priests is being efficiently realized when thus employed. We must recall afresh that the Gospel is primarily addressed to adults and that its proclamation to the younger members of the community is meaningful only if the adult pastorate is thriving.

Other questions also arise in our present situation. Is it really necessary to employ so many priests in diocesan administration? Must teachers of theology in our seminaries and universities be priests? Faced with questions such as these, we must first take a hard look at inherited attitudes, not to mention our prejudices. Would it not be much more sensible to leave such matters as building projects and finance to those lay members of the community professionally qualified to handle them? And the only thing that should disqualify a layman from teaching theology is lack of ability—not lack of ordination (in this connection we could learn from the Orthodox Church).

These are also the sort of questions we should ask when dividing manpower between the territorial and the non-territorial pastorate. Is what we have now gainfully employed, in the pastoral sense? Unfortunately the rough (German) statistics given above do not enable us to reach any clear conclusions. But the fact that, for example, in the diocese of Essen (see above) only 7% of all active priests are engaged in the non-territorial pastorate properly so called (hospitals, armed forces, prisons, special projects) is probably true for other dioceses. And 7% is just not enough! In her continuing insistence on administering a territorially structured pastorate, the Church runs the serious risk of making no impact at all in other significant areas of our highly differentiated society—the risk, quite simply, of not being present. Thus it is a gross folly, but nevertheless a fact, that in one diocese two full-time priests minister to the needs of a university community of about 8,000 Catholics, while in the same diocese 123 priests minister to 662 independent pastoral districts containing approximately 1,000 Catholics altogether, and to another 149 districts that between them total between 1,000 and 2,000 Catholics. This situation is made nonetheless scandalous

by the fact that a number of these small parishes are administered by priests who in normal circumstances would have retired
from active work. In this situation it is hardly surprising that our
future graduates make blistering comments on the Church and
her structures. Examples of this type could be multiplied, but
suffice it to say that the relationship of territorially to non-
territorially employed manpower is badly out of proportion, to
the detriment of the non-territorial pastorate.

IV

PART-TIME PRIESTS

In the present circumstances there is a real need for the part-
time priest. Though part-time priests would not constitute a complete answer to the priest shortage, they would make a significant
difference.

What Is Meant by "Part-Time Priest"?

By a part-time priest I mean a man of mature years [9] who
already holds down a job and who, having received holy orders,
places himself at the disposal of the local community after he has
finished work for the day, on Sunday mornings, and, later, when
he has retired from his job.[10] Thus I am not talking about
worker-priests who move to the factory floor after completing
their theological studies and receiving ordination, but rather the
opposite: adult men who, already active and settled as workers,
teachers, doctors, etc., subsequently accept ordination. (This system need not exclude the possibility of a priest completing his
theological studies and then learning a trade; however, such
cases would be exceptional.)

[9] Neither should we close our minds to the future possibility that
women, too, will be admitted; cf. E. Gössmann, "Women as Priests," in
Concilium 34 (1968), pp. 59-64.

[10] Cf. F. Klostermann, "Priesterbild und Priesterbildung—Überlegun-
gen für übermorgen," in Der Seelsorger 35 (1965), pp. 299-316, esp.
pp. 308f.

The Position of the Part-Time Priest

I do not wish to suggest that in the future there will be no need for full-time priests; in a society such as ours that is unimaginable. For large parishes and also for time-consuming duties in the non-territorial pastorate (universities, hospitals, etc.) the future will show a continuing need for full-time priests. But our present situation does require differentiated presbyteral categories. It would be fatal if we were to allow our historically-conditioned image of the presbyterate to blind us to every expression of its essence but the theologically qualified, full-time, celibate minister. And now that I have mentioned celibacy, let it be said at once that as long as this is obligatory, we might just as well forget the part-time priesthood (though the celibacy question is, of course, important in other respects, too). As F. Klostermann has observed: "It is to be assumed that neither the part-time diaconate nor the part-time presbyterate I am now suggesting will be limited to those willing to accept celibacy. Dispensation could readily be given, and in fact already has been, in the case of full-time priests (former Protestant ministers)." [11] Insistence on celibacy for the part-time priest would frighten off just the sort of people so urgently needed: mature, adult, married men competent in their chosen job who, by virtue of the abilities they have acquired in the course of their work, are well-suited to serve their communities.

As regards theological formation, we must free ourselves from the notion that advanced theological studies are absolutely necessary to the exercise of the presbyteral ministry. If married, part-time deacons can be authorized to preach without first having completed an exhaustive course in theology, it is difficult to see why a part-time priest could not also be dispensed from a full course. In short, the degree of theological education considered appropriate for the diaconate should also be sufficient for the part-time priesthood. As the German Bishops' Conference said in March 1968 when laying down norms for the training of dea-

[11] *Ibid.*

cons: "The theological education appropriate to a deacon will depend upon the disposition and standard of education of each candidate, his family background and his job, and also the particular diaconal function foreseen in his case. For men of mature age, study weeks or other such courses should be sufficient; alternatively, they might be given leave of absence from their jobs in order to be enrolled at a suitable institute. In certain cases a correspondence course might also be sufficient." [12]

Whatever else might be said on this matter, it is fair to say that a Church that can reintroduce a part-time married diaconate should find no serious obstacle to the introduction of a part-time presbyterate. Indeed, perhaps the deeper significance of the restoration of the diaconate will turn out to be an easing of the way toward a part-time, married presbyterate.

It might be objected at this point that a married family man taking on extra work of this type would be overburdening himself mentally and physically. This objection would need careful consideration in each particular case. On the other hand there is no reason to believe that there will be any appreciable lessening in the rate at which the time a man spends at his place of work is diminishing. Furthermore, it is surely possible that men who now spend much of their free time working for this or that charitable, social or political organization would be willing to place some of it at the disposal of the ecclesial community to which they belong. The workload here should be apportioned in accordance with the individual's ability and inclination.

Part-time priests would be particularly—though not of course exclusively—suited to work in the non-territorial pastorate. By virtue of their position in society and their experience of office and home, they would enjoy a more immediate contact with their fellow men. As Pius XI said in *Quadragesimo anno:* "Undoubtedly the first and immediate apostles of the workingmen must themselves be workingmen, while the apostles of the industrial and commercial world should themselves be employers and merchants" (n. 141). It is also worth noting that a society

[12] *Guiding Principles for the Formation of Deacons,* March 1968.

that produced and elected its own priests, whether from the factory floor, academic community, etc., would simply be revitalizing an ancient Christian tradition. Such a system would also have the incidental advantage of placing no additional financial burden on the local Church.

In this connection, n. 21 of Vatican Council II's *Decree on the Pastoral Office of Bishops in the Church* should also be considered: "When diocesan bishops, and others regarded in law as their equals, have become less capable of fulfilling their duties properly because of the increasing burden of age or some other serious reason, they are earnestly requested to offer their resignation from office either on their own initiative or upon invitation from the competent authority" (n. 21). In the *Motu Proprio Ecclesiae sanctae* (August 6, 1966) the age limit is set at 75. Logically, the same requirement should apply to the presbyterate. In other words, we should come to think of the episcopal and presbyteral ministries not exclusively as a lifetime task but, under certain conditions, as ministries exercised over a certain maximum period. This outlook could be important to a part-time priest who might well feel that, "because of the increasing burden of age or some other serious reason", he should resign his ministry.

It is greatly to be hoped that serious thought will be given to this matter of a part-time presbyterate. Given the ever-increasing priest shortage its introduction could be of real assistance, while also providing an opportunity of appreciably narrowing the gap between the pastorate as a whole and the world within which it works. In any event, the shortage of priests will force the Church to undertake structural reforms. Perhaps it is precisely emergency situations of this sort, crying out for remedial action, that give us grounds for hope that a reform will be carried through.

Augustin Andreu-Rodrigo/*Valencia, Spain*

The Relationship of the Diocesan Clergy to Religious Orders and Secular Institutes

I

ONE MEDIATOR AND MANY MINISTERS

The decisive point to be borne in mind concerning the various forms of ministry within the Church is that the role of Christ is primary and that they take their origin from it. His priesthood is made present and functions within the Church in a way that is organically ordered (with an order based on the descending scale of derivative functions: episcopate, priesthood and the various types of *diakonia*) and adapted to the needs of the community. This adaptation is demanded by the multiplicity of charisms or vocations within it, and by the resultant multiplicity of the situations in which the faithful can be placed.

These factors establish the *raison d'être* of every form of ministry. It is not just any people that is in view; it is the People *of God*. The priesthood above all is not to be understood in "monolithic" terms, as if "every priest were obliged to take a direct and active part in all the functions of the pastoral ministry",[1] or as if, when called on to fulfill some priestly function, he were forced to take up some predetermined and unchangeable position. There exists a *monastic* priesthood because there are monastic com-

[1] G. Frénaud, "Vie monastique et Sacerdoce," in *Gregorianum* 48 (1967), p. 595.

munities.[2] There exists a *religious* priesthood because there are religious communities. There exists a *secular institute* priesthood because there are secular institute communities. (Vatican Council II directed that from these latter communities some brother should be chosen to be ordained for their service [*Decree on the Renewal of Religious Life,* n. 10]. Religious and secular priests have no right to see in this a vote of no confidence.) There exists a *secular* priesthood because there are secular communities.

The priesthood, taken in the concrete, as a ministry, is not a species of consecration in the abstract but one destined for a particular situation,[3] and as such it has its form determined for it by the *type* of community to whose service it is destined; from the sociological point of view, it is something that arises from within the community and at the deepest level is homogeneous with it.

There is no particular type of community that has any grounds or right to consider itself the typical Christian community, with the heavenly Church as its antitype. The typical community is the Church herself. Speaking of societies that lead the common life, J. Beyer observes that "within the Church every society ought to enjoy freedom to be that which it is. It cannot be forced to assume a structure that does not correspond to its life, its function and its mission".[4] Every type of community is charismatic. Every community has the duty to think out its own particular charism here and now.[5] The relationship between these various communities and forms of life is not one of *assimilation* but of *collaboration* and convergence in the *one* Lord. The problems of a particular community are also those of all others, and the crisis of the religious life and of certain apostolic societies has

---

[2] G. Frénaud does not use this line of argument to justify the ordination of all monks.

[3] P. Schoonenberg, "Quelques reflexions sur le sacrement de l'ordre, en particulier sur le caractere sacramentel," in *Bulletin d'Informations de l'Institut pour l'Entraide Sacerdotale en Europe. Le pretre et le monde secularise* (Maastricht, 1968), p. 59.

[4] J. Beyer, "Les societes de vie commune," in *Gregorianum* 48 (1967), p. 748.

[5] J. Beyer, *art. cit.,* pp. 753ff.

to be seen in the context of their search for their charism in the world of today.[6] Secularity is also a charism. Its implications can no longer be thought out in the light of those religious and monastic analogies that have weighed on secular life ever since the 11th century.[7]

II
THE SECULAR COMMUNITY

The secular community is the fundamental one (A. Mirgeler). It is the Church within which a man receives existence as a Christian, the Church with the capacity for begetting an inexhaustible variety of particular communities and which, by that same token, is not organized around any *one* of these determinate forms with its particular ends or means.

Religious or para-religious communities are types of community characterized by their relative *uniformity* of timetable, dress, age (no children or adolescents), state, sex, religious devotions and, above all, by their selection of particular *means* for personal sanctification and the apostolate—of means, because the sanctity to which we are all called is one and the same. But the secular community is not uniform; it contains within itself every sort of diversity—of age (children, adolescents, adults, old people), of state (celibate, bachelor, married, widows), of cultural and economic levels, of function (rulers and ruled, buyers and sellers, patients and doctors), of sex, and so on. The secular community is not one that *has not chosen* to be a monastic or religious or secular institute; it simply *has chosen* to be secular. It is the people called into the desert; it is the assembly and council of

---

[6] F. Wulf, "¿Necesita aun la Iglesia de los religiosos?" in *Academia teologica* 4 (Salamanca, 1967), pp. 113-39, and in *Theologische Akademie* 4 (Frankfurt am M., 1967).

[7] A. Mirgeler, "Der Verlust der transzendenten Sinnfrage. Zum innerkirchlichen Verhaltnis zwischen Klerus und Laien," in *Hochland* 59 (1967), pp. 568-74; idem, "Monch und Laie," in *Hochland* 60 (1968), pp. 397-408.

God,[8] the instrument of salvation, the call of God. It has at its disposal the means adapted to its sanctification and apostolate. "The great community, divine in origin and perfect with a perfection still to be won, is the Holy Roman Catholic Church." [9] The problem is, whether this secular community is recognized as possessing full Christian citizen rights (without any *a priori* theorizing about an anthropology of castes) and whether, as a corollary, there is a priesthood that is and ought to be homogeneous with the secular community: the secular priesthood.

The secular community "lives in the world, that is to say, in each and every profession and occupation, as in the ordinary circumstances of family and social life with which its life is, as it were, interwoven. That is the context within which each man is called by God to fulfill his own task, with the spirit of the Gospel as his guide, in such a way that, like leaven, he may contribute from within to the sanctification of the world" (*Constitution on the Church,* n. 31). The secular community is bound up with all the ordinary circumstances of social life, present to every variety of life in the world; there are communities in rural, urban, suburban, underdeveloped, "ghetto", displaced, pre-industrial, industrial and post-industrial areas. The secular community identifies itself with the autonomous experience of the world—with its faith in God the creator and Savior as its starting point—in order to give the world the value that belongs to it, constructing the world in accordance with its own internal laws.

III

THE SECULAR PRIEST

It follows that the secular priest has to make his own the vocation of the secular community to which he belongs. His way of life, his position within civil society, his relationship to those

[8] H. Küng, *Estructuras de la Iglesia* (Barcelona, 1965), pp. 25ff.; *Strukturen der Kirche* (Freiburg im Br., 1964); *Structures of the Church* (London, 1968).

[9] A. Rodilla, *Sacerdocio Secular* (Valencia, 1965), p. 110.

goods conventionally called "material", his way of existing and serving within the community—none of these can be deduced from the typology of the priest, as given by the history of religions, including the Jewish religion, or from "religious" ways of life that appeared before the modern experience of a world that is hominized and can be humanized.[10] The secular priest feels it as a species of alienation when he is interrogated from the standpoint of the "states of perfection" and foresees it as his immediate task to reintegrate himself into the conditions of his secular community; his desire is to serve the concrete secular vocation of this particular people.

1. *The community life* proper to the secular priest is life in and with the secular community whose minister he is and in the company of other ministers who are not priests. The state of preventive isolation in which secular priests have lived was the fruit, on the one hand, of a concern for asceticism, and, on the other, of a desire to see a form of priestly community that would allow priests to be classified in terms of an analogy with religious; operating in the background was a caste-conception of the priesthood, helped along by the oblivion into which the homogeneous priestly status of the people had fallen.[11] The community of the priest is that within which he ceases to be dangerously alone. It is not possible for the community to be a danger to him who is its minister. For secular priests to be grouped and to live together at a given place or time can only have the same motives as those which make doctors live in at hospitals or teachers at schools—motives that are functional or ministerial.

For the rest, the priesthood is not a means to the individual sanctification of bishop and priests; it is simply the governing portion of the secular diocesan community. It is an integral part of the secular community, an organism of ministry, neither an *en soi* nor a *pour soi*. Once the priesthood is considered from the

[10] J.-B. Metz, "Die Zukunft des Glaubens in einer hominisierten Welt" in *Hochland* 56 (1964), pp. 377ff.; H. Schlette, "Reflexions au sujet de la secularisation," in *Bulletin* . . . , pp. 4ff.

[11] O. Semmelroth, "The Priestly People of God and Its Official Ministers," in *Concilium* 31 (1968), pp. 87-100.

standpoint of ministry or function, "there disappear both the grounds for its isolation and those for its status as an exception in the midst of the faithful. [The priest] is called to holiness, but not to a holiness distinct from that of every one of the faithful. That is why the priesthood as such cannot be the ground for arguments in favor of special forms of dress, prayer, way of life or state of life (celibacy)".[12] In the secular community the priest will one day find as great a coherence, fraternal life and flexibility as in uniform communities. The present operational underdevelopment of diocesan communities gives no idea of the coherence and unity of purpose they could have.

The possibility that a priest might belong to the secular community, and be under the authority of someone who need not be the bishop, is greeted with well-justified reserve. Charisms can and ought to complete each other, but need not always be piled on top of one another.

2. *In the secular community* there are bachelors, celibates, married people, widows and widowers, all of them involved in the same evangelical vocation within the world. If a secular community needs one of its members—a married man, a widower, a celibate or a bachelor—to be a minister or a priest, there seem to be no grounds on which this could be denied to it. All are together bound to the same eucharistic morality and the same Gospel, and it must be possible to serve the Gospel from within any secular situation—professional, economic, cultural or sacramental (baptized, or baptized and married). "The desire for marriage, if it be genuinely rooted in the Lord, can lead to a link between priesthood and marriage that could be as salutary for the Church and the world as the link between ministry and celibacy." [13]

3. *Secular obedience,*[14] the *type* of the obedience of the secu-

[12] F. Haarsma, "Quelques theses sur la theologie pastorale chez le pretre," in *Bulletin* . . . , p. 120.

[13] P. Schoonenberg, *art. cit.*, p. 62.

[14] G. Rambaldi, "Docilita allo Spirito Santo, liberta dei figli di Dio e obbedienza del presbitero secondo il decreto 'Presbyterorum Ordinis'," in *Gregorianum* 48 (1967), pp. 481-521.

lar priest, arises from the structure and conditions of a vocation within the world. The attempt to find grounds in the *promitto* of the Ritual for reading into it a vow is lacking in any sort of consistency.[15] The foundation of secular obedience cannot leave on one side the secular community itself. Obedience within the priesthood, obedience of the faithful to their priest and of the faithful to their bishop, *has a permanent character of dialogue* (*Decree on the Ministry and Life of Priests,* n. 15). The professionalization of all ministries within the Church [16] demands collaboration with all other professions that are dedicated to constructing, scientifically and technically, the new human city. The priest's obedience is one with an initiative whose guiding principle is charity (*ibid.*). Dialogue obedience is obedience to God in the measure that it is a mutual obedience. It is very often a prophetic obedience.

Dialogue obedience produces unity and cohesion through the mechanism of *our daily covenant,* the eucharist, because a dialogue with no covenant is as immoral as a covenant with no dialogue. The bishop at all times has the last word among his priests, and the same is true of the priest in his community, but this last word is only the last if everyone else has had his word too (*Constitution on the Church in the Modern World,* nn. 15, 31).[17]

4. *The secular community* is not one in which a lesser generosity or greater selfishness is allowed or tolerated than in specialized communities. It is just that the hierarchy of values imposed by the makeup of the community is different.[18] *Secular poverty* has to be judged in the context of the given social structures, and no secular Christian can content himself with being "spiritually" poor if that does not include a determination to promote as *effec-*

[15] A. Aubry, "A propos de la signification du 'Promitto'," in *Nouv. Rev. Theol.* 85 (1963), pp. 1063-68.

[16] O. Schreuder, *Gestaltwandel der Kirche* (Freiburg im Br., 1967), pp. 81-99.

[17] F. Klostermann, "Perspectives de theologie pastorale," in *Bulletin* . . . , p. 101.

[18] J.-M. González-Ruiz, *El Cristianismo no es un humanismo* (Madrid, 1966), pp. 156ff.

tively as possible a structural distribution of wealth—this being over and above the many other forms of help that must be given to your neighbor, whether you seek him out or he, in his need, seeks out you. The morality of the secular community can be nothing other than that of the eucharist.[19] If people do not advert to the fact that the evangelical counsels are simply *a particular set of means* to the fulfillment of the precepts, they fall into the error of simply regulating competing egoisms and "abandon that attitude which is indivisibly scientific and humanist to settle down comfortably in the myth of an absolute truth" (R. Garaudy)[20] —in this case, the myth of the sacredness of property.

The secular priest wants to own property and use money, just as his community owns property and uses money. He wants to earn and to consume. Money gained in secular occupations (*Decree on the Ministry and Life of Priests,* n. 8) is the money most appropriate to the hands of the secular priest. The absence of any sort of earning, made in terms of work with a recognized value in the human city, cannot be justified *simply* by his consecration as a priest.

The ascetical values present in this form of poverty are undeniable. The secular priest does not want a privileged kind of security against the future, nor does he want an inalienable right to claim the provision of all he needs from the bishop; he wants his own position to be in no way at an advantage over that of the secular community, which is his community. For that reason it is a matter of urgency to abandon all that survives of the symbolic and privileged cocoon of tithes and dues to the clergy. In the eyes of a secular community, only that priest who is correspondingly secular will have any sort of credibility. For him, secularity is the way of perfection.

[19] A. Rodilla, *op. cit.,* p. 112.
[20] *Marxisme du XXe siecle* (Paris, 1966), pp. 16ff.

Karl Rahner, S.J./*Münster, West Germany*
Karl Lehmann/*Mainz, West Germany*

The Role of Priests
in a World of Revolution

INTRODUCTION

The time when priests enjoyed a direct and powerful influence on politics is gone, at least in most countries, even though there is still a considerable amount of flotsam and jetsam drifting about. Nevertheless, Richelieu is definitely dead. At the same time, we have overcome for the greater part those kinds of spiritual enthusiasm that wanted to limit Christianity and the Church's mission exclusively to the cult of a wholly interior piety. A new, purified and better informed—and therefore also "critical"—attitude toward political realities in the broad sense is emerging. And while politics and salvation are not identical, one cannot say either that the one begins where the other leaves off.

If we want to clarify the image of the priest today, we cannot ignore these questions. At the moment there is no chance that a "theoretical" treatment could provide us with a valid concept; it would moreover contradict to a certain extent the highly con- crete and practical reality with which we are here concerned. One can perhaps only talk about this insofar as one is "com- mitted". We have tried to find a way out (on the whole good and legitimate) by seeking opinions from the various regions of the world. The question put was: *What kind of specific part should the priest play with regard to the problems of the "third world" of the developing countries and toward revolutionary tendencies in individual countries?* During the last months this question has become even more urgent.

Despite great efforts by the General Secretariat and a definite promise, we unfortunately were unsuccessful in obtaining a requested contribution on this subject from Latin America. We profoundly regret that the promised article had not yet reached us by the required deadline.

THE PRIEST'S ROLE IN AN INDUSTRIAL CIVILIZATION

Marie-Dominique Chenu O.P., Paris, France

Prophecy before Evangelization

The effective life of the Church as the hierarchical community of the People of God is the immediate theological source (*locus theologicus*) of the understanding of the faith in practice. This methodological principle holds particularly when we want to determine the theology, pastoral situation and sociological position of the priest in this society of the 20th century. Hence the need for a sociological and theological analysis of this meeting point between Church and society in time and space in the various sectors of the Church and according to the various civilizations.

I

Where Western Europe is concerned, here are *some major facts which must be objectively accepted before we start interpreting.* The most striking fact is that of the *worker-priests,* particularly in France and Belgium between 1946 and 1958. We are not concerned here with their history, their development, their evangelical success or their ecclesiastical lack of success, and then their revival in 1966 after Vatican Council II. Beyond these episodes, what matters is the initiative. It is this that is meaningful, recognized today, proclaimed and further worked out. This raised, implicitly and bluntly, the question of the Church's relations with the world in a mankind profoundly transformed by our industrial civilization. The Church was, in a sense, forced to come out and become "missionary".

After the Council more and more priests in different European countries began to undertake, with the implicit or explicit consent of their bishops, *"professional" work* as engineers, economists, lawyers, etc., particularly where new social relationships developed, thus weaving that human fabric which provides a new meaning to the evangelical notion of the "neighbor".

The same inspiration and similar conditions led *a fair number of priests to take up a secular wage-paying part-time job while keeping on the sacred functions of the traditional ministry.* An inquiry conducted among priests in the rural sector revealed that 48 percent of them foresaw that in the future they would have to work manually or as simple technicians.

In the matter of training and preparation for the priesthood, practically everywhere it is *accepted not only as useful but as an advantage that seminarians and novices spend prolonged periods in secular enterprises,* according to their ability.

In the course of the occasionally violent episodes in the evolution of the economic structures, *the clergy,* and sometimes the bishops, *have publicly taken up a semi-revolutionary position* which, thirty years ago, would have been considered unthinkable and even blameworthy. The axiom that "the priest does not engage in politics", proclaimed everywhere for a century, has not been discarded today, but nevertheless it has been subjected to a sharp revision, with all the problems and risks this entails.

II

Let us now move on to *the sociological, pastoral and theological interpretation of these facts, according to innumerable reports and inquiries conducted by groups of priests themselves.*

First of all, this challenging of the definition and the various functions of the priest is clearly *linked with the Church's renewal,* inspired by the Council. It is normal that an ecclesiology *transformed by a return to the Gospel and by the demand for relevance to the present* will cause people to dispute hieratic forms of behavior and the pastoral forms of the sacerdotal ministry.

At the heart of this evolution there lies *obviously severe criticism of a "Christian establishment"* and, as it is called, the "Constantinian" Church—i.e., a Church where the apostolic ministry leans on the structures and prestige of the economic, social and political regime as the normal vehicle for pastoral work. The secularization of society and the inevitable and, in principle, beneficent effect of industrialization as the way toward the control of the forces of nature have led to a revaluation of the categories of "sacred" and "profane". Priority is given to the mystery of Christ as recapitulating all truth and all values, in a sanctification which does not imply "sacralization" as was the case in Christianity. As a logical consequence of this christological dynamism, the clergy tend to shake off the caste mentality, more inspired by the levitical priesthood of the Old Testament than by the new covenant. And so they no longer undertake secular work in order to "sacralize" it but in order to show forth there the presence of the Church in the world, within the autonomy of earthly values. It is on these lines that one should understand that sometimes clumsy process of "de-clericalization", from the question of wearing the cassock to the will no longer to live like people of eminence and privilege. The priest is chosen, "set apart", by his calling, but he is not "separated"; he is a man among men, like Christ.

Driven by this same inspiration, *the priest,* thus committed, *attaches a major importance to his prophetic role* as the instrument with which the Gospel challenges the established order in an evolutionary or revolutionary world. And so he reduces the share allotted to functions of worship and hieratic sensibilities which exist only within the community of believers. He must prophesy before evangelizing, evangelize before catechizing, catechize before sacramentalizing; these are the stages through which he must act, and in this order.

The *criterium* for the evangelical value and ecclesial efficacy of this activity *lies in the encounter with the poor,* an encounter which must be as spontaneous as possible. This is not just the theme of a moralizing sermon but the sign *par excellence* of the coming of the Messiah. Here we discover, in an affluent society, the betrothal between St. Francis and Lady Poverty, by which the *Poverello* denounced in his day the evils of the feudal society sacralized by the Church. In order to be genuine this love of the poor must imply the battle for justice, right through the ambiguities of all kinds of emancipation, including those of the "third world".

THE SITUATION IN SPAIN

Ildefonso Alvarez Bolado, S.J., Madrid, Spain

Taken as it stands, the problem stated in this article seems to me ambiguous, particularly when considered in the context of the present situation of the Spanish Church. Is it possible to consider within a single perspective "the" attitude (whether positive, negative or "detached") of the priest to the "revolution"? Have we an even remotely clear idea of what it means *sociologically* to be a priest in our society in process of secularization, shaped by fundamental historical changes, objectively "pluralist" with a pluralism that reaches into the depths of the Church herself? I cannot see that we have. And it seems to me too soon for any total confrontation of the Church (as the People of God) with our contemporary world that is determined by the fact of, the values implied by, and the emotions bound up with the "revolution factor". Only through that dialogue within the Church which must arise from this confrontation of the People of God with its historical world will there be worked out that complex of many-sided attitudes which the priest, in the service of all Christian communities, can adopt toward the "revolutionary factor" in our culture. This process seems to lead inevitably to a change in the sociological "status" of the priest within the Church and consequently outside her.

The Meaning and Purpose of Dialogue within the Church

When we say that the question has to be settled by a dialogue within the Church—one which has not yet begun in Spain—we are not thinking of a solipsistic dialogue of the Church with herself; the Church is unceasingly in dialogue with the world and with the realities of the world which have a charismatic potentiality of meaning that has to be discarded by the community of faith. In this dialogue within the Church on the modern world and the factors shaping it, much more of a hearing has to be given—by the Church as an institution—to the Christian *laity*. Only a laity genuinely listened to in such a dialogue will bring into focus the rich and objective pluralism of the forces shaping the modern world and also make possible that pluralism which arises from the legitimate self-determination of local churches, a pluralism which the Church cannot sidestep in her progress toward taking her place in the world. The price of failing to achieve this would be to perpetuate within the Church the dominance of the "clerical" outlook. It makes no difference in that case whether we have to deal with "establishment clericalism" or "revolutionary clericalism", or with the fatal outcome of that dichotomy, the inevitable clash between "right-wing clericalism" and "left-wing clericalism". The real problem is quite different: to free the entire People of God to take its place as a pluralist reality in the historical world and to make the priest not a clerical stereotype of the left or the right, but the servant of the People in this process, so that faith may be its beginning and its end.

The Clerical Church

The ambiguity of the question as considered within our national context arises from a peculiar radicalization of those factors, already mentioned, that make for confusion. Our priesthood goes on being a sociological caste and, in consequence, our Church is still slavishly clerical, with a laity granted no access to dialogue within the Church. Our Church is one with no officially recognized interior pluralism, possessing only a "clandestine" pluralism. As a result, the revolutionary movements genuinely existing within our society are incapable of receiving the treatment due to them in the dialogue within the Church, and their reflection within the Church is therefore in the form of "underground schisms" which gravely handicap the Church in her mission of evangelization. This is especially true for those communities dedicated to evangelizing the world of the workers and that of the universities. Pastors and militants alike often find themselves placed as Christians in situations of painful ambiguity.

The Relationship between Church and State

The key to this ambiguity—at any rate, the most obvious one —is to be found in the present juridical dispensation that governs relationships between Church and State. In this situation, which seems an anachronistic denial of the pluralism proper to every modern society, the tendency of the State is efficiently to stifle every beginning of pluralism within the Church, no matter how slight; after all, the official recognition of such a pluralism would call into question the very existence of such a State that conceives of itself as the exclusive representative of a national unanimity. The Church, for her part, tends to take advantage of the established Catholicism of the State in order to eradicate whatever pluralism—whether religious, ideological or political —might tend to destroy her "official" role in the social life of the country. In this way the "concordat" that regulates the present relationship of Church and State perpetuates simultaneously a mutual control of each over the other through the reciprocal granting of privilege; this grant is made by the Church to the present form of the State by conferring on it the dignity of a "Catholic State", and by the State to the Church through the guarantee of her leading role in the country's historical life and by the official recognition of the Catholic faith as the established religion of the State. This situation is resented and denounced by the rapidly expanding minorities as an ideological relic of the past and an anachronistic superstructure.

A Free Church in Modern Society

Under these circumstances the Spanish Church should single-mindedly strive for the recovery of her internal pluralism, since only through such a pluralism will she be able to achieve a real relationship both with Spanish society and with the revolutionary tensions which exist in it. This pluralism is indispensable if we want to avoid a situation in which the believer's and the priest's compromise with the secular order draws us into a neo-Constantinianism, whether revolutionary or counter-revolutionary, or into a painful schism, whether open or clandestine.

In order to bring into being this new state of affairs, one so much more adapted to the Church's taking her place within Spanish society, it is imperative that the Church free herself from her present "union" with the State and demand no juridical "status" other than that of any legitimate human community. She will thereby achieve far greater solidarity with all other authentic human communities and no longer render them marginal by her preoccupation with the sociological "centrality" of the *temple*. For the *temple,* when it is a *politically* privileged place, is also the place in which the "established power" sets chains on the prophetic mission of the Church and on her "bias in favor of the poor of the earth". In modern society, if the Church insists on preserving her privileged "official" role within the "system", she cannot be the Church of all men. Nor, obviously, can she with untroubled mind think out her attitude when confronted with possible revolutionary tensions which, as they rise up against the "system", rise up necessarily against her also.

Our answer is therefore simple: In order to give an answer to the questions proposed, in order to face it squarely, *the Spanish Church must recover her inner pluralism and give recognition to that pluralism which already exists within her.*

THE PRIEST AND REVOLUTION IN AFRICA

James O'Connell, S.M.A., Zaria, Nigeria

The General Political Situation

Few things are surer in the African situation [1] than the likeli-hood of political revolutions in many countries during the next decade.[2] The governments of the new States took over a tenuous tradition of constitutional rule which they have often not re-spected and which their opponents have been equally willing to discard. Many independence settlements failed to come to terms with the real distribution of power among political groups, and attempts are inevitably made to find a better equilibrium among contending forces. Inexperienced governments were faced with situations where the socially awakened sectors of their popula-tions were eager for economic progress but where scarce natural resources, falling commodity prices and a scarcity of skills are making rapid economic growth well-nigh impossible. Countries that are multi-ethnic have had communal differences exacer-bated as educated members of different ethnic groups compete with one another for posts in the public services and various limited forms of patronage. Finally, in southern Africa, Portu-guese colonialism and white minority governments are defying the weight of numbers and the logic of de-colonization and de-mocracy in a precarious bid to hold on to power and privilege.

I

If many governments fall in Africa during the next decade—as many have already fallen—we shall have witnessed in most cases a *coup d'état* rather than a revolution. A *coup d'état* in-

---

[1] For practical purposes I have confined my observations to Black Africa, or Africa south of the Sahara. And since, in the course of a short article, generalizations have constantly to be made, it is well to keep in mind that there is a French saying: all generalizations, includ-ing this one, are false.

[2] On this problem of instability, see J. O'Connell, "The Fragility of Stability," in *Journal of Modern African Studies* 5 (1968), pp. 181-91.

volves a violent change of government but leaves the existing structures of society intact, whereas a revolution not only changes a government but changes society as well.[3] Yet in several African countries the recent coups express tensions, and particularly populist tensions, that may before long explode into revolutions. Events in the Congolese revolutions of the early 1960's made clear that the masses of the people had wanted changes in the structures of society at a moment when the elite groups had wanted only to transfer political authority from the Belgians to themselves. Events in other African countries suggest now that the aspirations and stresses that came to light in the Congo [4] are less exceptional than originally seemed to be the case.

The African Priests

· In the vicissitudes that countries have been going through, the reactions of African priests have been little different from those of secular elite groups. In countries like Dahomey, the Upper Volta and Nigeria, the priests were among those opposed to the flagrant corruption and flamboyant waste of the political classes, and they helped to generate the social climate in which the independence governments were brought down. In Ghana, Gabon and the Cameroon Republic, individual bishops and priests stood up bravely against injustices and defied the claims of autocratic governments. In the southern Sudan the priests shared the general resentment of the southern peoples against the Arabic and Islamic pressures of the northern-led government and inevitably took on a certain political leadership in the southern revolt. In southern Africa, and particularly in South Africa, southern Rhodesia, and the Portuguese territories, African priests have tended to stay apart from the political resistance movements. But they undoubtedly share the sentiments of the resistance groups. They have had their Christian faith tried by the evident willing-

[3] On the distinction between a "revolution" and a *"coup d'état"* see H. Seton-Watson, *Neither War nor Peace* (London, 1960), pp. 188-91.
[4] See H. Weiss, *Political Protest in the Congo* (Princeton, N.J., 1967), pp. xxii-xxiii, 291-92.

ness of the ecclesiastical authorities to collaborate with and support racist and repressive governments and by the indifference of Catholics elsewhere in the world.

II

In discussing priests in relation to politics and revolution in Africa, it is impossible to avoid the factor of ethnicity. In this respect Africa resembles central Europe in the period before World War I as well as many contemporary Asian countries. Ethnicity colors alignments in politics, allocation of amenities and competition for posts. It constantly plays a pervasive and obtrusive role that obscures the existence of other factors (such as the insecurity caused by the pace of social change, for example) that sharpen tribalist bitterness in countries where solidarity and defensiveness more easily take on ethnic forms than they do social class or other forms. Unfortunately very few members of the intelligentsia manage to rise above tribalism or the aggressive aspects of ethnicity. In those countries—Uganda, the Congo and Nigeria—where ethnic dissensions have erupted violently, priests have on a whole divided along ethnic lines. Yet it must be said to the credit of African priests that their views have been more moderate than those of other elite groups. In Nigeria the Ibo bishops were a powerful lobby for a solution less extreme than the final decision of the Ibo leadership to secede. The saddest result of tribalism is that it constantly falsifies the social issues that confront the peoples and leads them into artificial and unnecessary hostility toward one another.

The Reaction of Missionaries and Expatriate Foreign Priests

Expatriate priests who by and large had come to terms with the colonial governments had not been particularly well disposed toward the nationalist movements in the early days. But independence has brought them to the realization that they could work with the new governments and that their contributions in schools and hospitals were appreciated. They have tended to stand back from politics and have hesitated to speak out on social issues lest they be accused of being foreigners who were meddling with internal affairs. They have usually held much the same opinions on local politics as the indigenous elite groups among whom they worked. Sometimes their local allegiances have led them into implicit or explicit political positions, as when in Nigeria many Irish missionaries who worked among the Ibos supported their secession and those who worked among the other peoples favored the continuation of the federation. Bishops have made conventional clerical protests in some countries where governments threatened to take over religious school systems. One such confrontation led to the expulsion of a French-born archbishop from Guinea. But all foreign priests have since been expelled from that country where internal economic difficulties and the legacy of bitterness left by the departing French authorities made it easy to turn the missionaries into scapegoats.

Where expatriate or white priests have really failed in an African revolutionary situation is in southern Africa. In southern Rhodesia and South Africa the clergy have mostly either supported or done little to mitigate the racism of their lay people. Declarations in favor of African rights by bishops who did not even back them up by a proper allocation of priests and diocesan resources between white and black Catholics have done little to alter the general situation. Undoubtedly the Church in these lands will survive the poor social approach of her clerical leaders, since her religious message in spite of an inadequate social embodiment makes an impact on minds and hearts. But a Church whose priests are not more sensitive to the social logic of the faith and who are so obsessed with the problem of order that they turn a deaf ear to the exigencies of justice is an impoverished one.

III

The New Concept of the Priest

What is the role of a priest in a revolutionary or potentially revolutionary situation? This question takes on a particular significance not only in the immediate African circumstances but in

times where a new concept of a priest is gradually being formu-
lated. Here there is space only to put forward some general considerations:

1. Though he belongs to the elite groups through his education, the priest is linked by his representative functions to his
entire community, and particularly to the "poor of God" who are
so easily forgotten by the powerful. A priest cannot be party to
or acquiesce in any political solution that does not seek justice
for all the people. In addition, he needs to make use of his education and influence to articulate and advocate the rights of the
people.

2. His mediating role sets the priest to bridge the divisions
between men. There is neither Jew nor Greek nor any other
people as he stands with his community before God. No man
more than the priest is bound to seek political integration within
a State and to reject tribalist stereotypes and oppositions.

3. If the Church needs a minimum freedom to carry on her
mission, this freedom itself is a symbol of all the human freedoms
that belong to God and not to Caesar. Priests who truly cherish a
universal concern not only exercise a vigilance over ecclesiastical
rights but bear witness to all forms of human freedom.

4. A priest preaches the Gospel in his witness of the Word
and in his integrity of life. More often than not his action on the
political sphere is indirect. But as the Gospel permeates men's
consciences it exercises a profoundly humanizing influence. And
in the long run there are no forces more revolutionary than the
logic of Christian ideas and the power of Christian actions.

5. A priest is no man of violence. Neither is any other good
man. At best, violence is a last resort. It can be chosen only as a
lesser evil, when the other choice is gross human exploitation and
abject submission. Yet when men choose violence, a priest may
at times have to acknowledge that the implications of his preaching and the manner in which he kept company with men has
served to lead toward this result. He may himself have no choice
but to go along with it. But on him more than on others falls the
obligation to mitigate the inevitable evils of violence.

6. In a world that has rapidly grown extremely de-sacralized, the priest loses his previous place among those of established authority. Yet he may find himself instead in the role of a secular leader. Those young priests who joined revolutionaries in Latin America evidently accepted this change. They broke from concepts of a separated clerical (as distinct from priestly) state to throw themselves into a violent struggle that sought justice against established authority. Should the priesthood be conferred on married men of secular attainments—as may well happen soon in Africa—this issue of leadership will become even more acute.

7. In the last resort the priest takes his sacred character from functions that leave him in the world and yet draw him apart. He presides over worship, he bears witness to the Gospel, and he labors to build a community of love. Whatever else he does must not only leave these functions intact but also relate logically to them.

THE PRIEST AND MINORITY GROUPS

Robert Fox, New York, N.Y.

There are a number of problems facing the priest whose mission is to a minority group. Recognized and confronted, these problems can lead to a profound experience of priesthood and a relevant ministry. If they are avoided or ignored, however, the result can be bitter frustration for the individual or an unfounded sense of accomplishment. In this article, I shall discuss several of these problems and then briefly present a sense of the priesthood that has resulted from my efforts to confront them.

Lack of Respect

The first concerns the lack of respect for minority groups which exists everywhere in the world—the overwhelming failure to really look at minority groups and the people who compose them and to see their potential and their riches. The priest is as affected by this lack of respect and failure to see as anyone else because, consciously or unconsciously, he shares the prejudices of the majority group—from which he generally comes or to which he has been grafted in his formation. Thus he needs to grapple with this prejudice and to be in touch with this instinctual negative reaction to the minority groups. Highly motivated priests steeped in intellectualized values tend to repress any consciousness of personal prejudice. The result is a restricted ability to truly experience the minority group, which is expressed either in low expectation or in simplistic overidentification. Either posture generates crippling paternalism.

In his own belief in an immanent God, the priest should find the basis for a deep respect for the people with whom he is working—respect for them as persons, for their culture, for the circumstances that confront them and for their reactions to their whole life-experience. If he understands his priesthood as a call of a living, immanent God to come from everyone and everything he experiences, he will be less inclined to impose his values and reactions upon the people. His own growth and becoming will be the stimulus toward formation for his people and the best possible witness to the presence and availability of the living God.

Embracing and maintaining such a posture is not at all easy. Within every man there exists the tendency to get above it all, a tendency that springs from a resistance to the struggle that life or reality asks of a man. This is pronounced in the person who chooses a role of service to the rest of men, because service can so easily be twisted to generate a sense that the other has a need which I do not share. Certainly the priest is tempted in this direction. Moreover, since the same resistance to life is found in the people, there exists on their part a tendency to accede to or even demand a figure who will offer and provide a way out. So even if the priest is conscious of his need to avoid drawing the people "upward" toward himself, he must go further and resist the pressure of the people to make of him a special kind of person with the key to escape in this life or in the next. Finally, this process of a deeper and deeper penetration of life is pursued only at the price of continued self-discovery, and that entails an experience of one's poverty as well as one's riches. The priest's tendency to conceive himself as a model for his people renders any experience of his personal poverty almost intolerable. Despite frequent protestations of sinfulness in the liturgy, the priest can be actually impervious to any experience of that fact. To the extent that he is, his ability to confront life is restricted.

The Problem of Identification

This leads to a consideration of another problem facing the priest who has a mission to a minority group. With all their experience of unlikely living circumstances, prejudice and frustration, the people must be nonetheless confronted with the challenge of celebrating themselves, which necessitates the kind of identification with self that at once illustrates and generates a true experience of freedom and love. For a people in struggle, appearances frequently seem to eliminate any consideration of celebration. Celebration is then either ignored or experienced as an esoteric rite seen to be desirable insofar as it prescinds from and "transcends" the lives of the people.

In challenging the people to experience life, even to the extreme of celebrating themselves as they unfold at life's hands, the priest becomes both for himself and the people the object of resistance. For himself because he will spontaneously resist the experiences of self that life makes possible: self as poor in so many ways, self as embracing positions that challenge his own society, self as enigma to family and friends, self as rejected by many who consider him as dangerous, self as rich in so many ways. For the people because they will spontaneously resist the experience of themselves which their life circumstances offer them. The priest must consistently fulfill this role of celebrant even when the people he serves and he himself are in turn scorned, pitied or "helped", and such attitudes of society are intensely productive for his growth as a priest. However, equally intense is the pressure to reject that role in favor of an apparently more relevant service, that of liberating the people from the untenable circumstances in which they find themselves. Liberation, of course, is man's destiny, but the Son of Man liberates through a deep incarnation in human experience in which man grows at once in his capacity for vulnerable self-discovery and his capacity to celebrate the person he is discovering. Any cause of liberation which holds up a mythical better life (whether in this world or the next) as an alternative to a dying-living engagement in the stuff of current reality is serving idols and not the living God.

Frequently the question has been asked whether the priest whose mission is to a cultural group other than his own can or should divest himself of his culture to assume that of the group he serves. The unfortunate assumption implied in this question is that a man can be defined or circumscribed by a culture. As they flinch in the face of life's growth-producing impetus, members of a minority group can substitute retreat into cultural forms for authentic reaction to current reality. Their priest can deceive himself by weighing the advantages of hiding behind a static image of himself delineated by his own cultural forms or that of the people, all the while missing the real issue of authentic self-discovery at the hands of the experience confronting him.

To give an example: as black men in the United States struggle to a discovery of who they are, hairstyles, music and typical foods are readily available, but such are inadequate answers. Conscious experience of prejudice and discrimination, awareness of the illness of racism even at the price of experiencing oneself as its object, knowing oneself to be undesirable to the majority, and all of this integrated with an ever intensifying celebration of self in the context of gratuitous faith and love—these are the true issues involved in the black man's self-discovery. The priest who serves Negroes fails if he conceives of his role as either that of simply identifying with their cultural forms or seducing them to his. Similarly he fails if he sees his function as opening ways for their incorporation into the mainstreams of American life. Martin Luther King Jr. clearly understood this and forcefully lived a true leadership and a true priesthood. His life was given to a deep penetration of reality, an intense consciousness of himself in every experience and a continuing peace or celebration of self. Because this was so, he became an organic agent leading his people to a confrontation with life-circumstances that a man would ordinarily shun. Those who followed him, both black and white, have experienced power in powerlessness, security in vulnerability and peace in the conflict generated by truth.

The Required Qualities

Three qualities seem necessary for the priest who has a mission to a minority group—and, indeed, for every priest:

The *first* of these is a reflectiveness born of an all-embracing respect for all that exists—from people to things to issues. His belief in a living God, who has gone to the pains to create and redeem in order to make himself available to men, keeps the priest off-balance enough to pursue the mystery of God in the unlikely as well as the likely.

The *second* is a responsiveness in which the priest allows himself to become a conscious name for whatever he experiences and so names himself in the process. Not a static impersonal name invulnerably circumscribed by verbalism, but a dynamic, personal and ever changing name. A name now lettered in tears and then in laughter, sweat, joy, failure, success, fear, comradeship, loneliness. His responsibility for the Word of God goes far beyond preaching an intellectualized dogma to embrace, so that it will become a living Word.

The *third* quality is a commitment to relationship through which the priest consistently strives to experience himself in the other and encourage the other to experience himself in him. The black man is neither his ward nor his cause but rather the image of himself in whom he discovers his own doubts about belonging. The prostitute is neither his case nor his campaign but rather the incarnation of his own sale of self. The saint is neither his idol nor his reproach but rather a challenge to experience the riches within him. Thus his approach to the growth of community is neither legal nor manipulative. It is organic in that in his person he becomes the ground in which he and men discover one another as unique, distinct and yet, nonetheless, one.

If it seems from what I have written that every man is charged with priesthood, it is my conviction that this is so and that the ordained priest is not meant to be a priest for men but rather lives his priesthood to hasten men along the path to theirs.

PART II
BIBLIOGRAPHICAL SURVEY

Karl Rahner, S.J./*Münster, West Germany*
Karl Lehmann/*Mainz, West Germany*

The Discussion
on Celibacy

INTRODUCTION

When we planned this volume, the question of how to deal
with the debate on celibacy gave us cause for considerable concern. The comprehensive nature of the problem prevented us
from dealing with it in one single article. (Later on a special
volume with contributions from various departments of *Concilium* might be possible.) Moreover, such a single article would
not have suited the different situations which obtain in different
countries.

The proposal to bring the real issue to the fore via a comprehensive and informative report on the debate about celibacy was
welcomed explicitly by the Executive Editorial Committee at the
conferences of the editors of *Concilium* at Paris and Madrid in
1967 and 1968, and it was agreed that this was the best way of
meeting the present state of the discussion and the requirements
of this publication.

It was therefore the aim of the Bibliographical Survey to put
together and document the most varied positive and negative
tendencies, arguments and aspects of this problem as they appear
in literature, public opinion and some less public discussions.
This would then result in a practical survey of the reasons for
and against celibacy.

Unfortunately we were unable to obtain this information from

all countries. Authors whom we found, after much trouble, had
to inform us after a while that they could not fulfill their commitment because the competent authorities had informed them that
the subject was taboo and refused to let it be discussed freely in
public. Priests who did so despite such warnings were suspended
or relieved from their posts. This happened particularly in the
Philippines. Similar experiences, although less dramatic, were reported to us from Asiatic missionary countries. The situation in
countries of Eastern Europe is very peculiar. A report, promised
from Yugoslavia, was withdrawn shortly before the deadline
with the expression of the hope "that we would understand the
situation". Another country from Eastern Europe sent us the
following reply: "The subject is extraordinarily difficult and
practically taboo here. The difficulty arises primarily from the
fact that up till now practically nothing has appeared on this
subject. . . . There are only a few articles that emphasize the
sacrosanct spiritual values of celibacy. To doubt or criticize it
would, in our peculiar situation, be viewed almost as treason.
The problem is not ripe for discussion here. This does not mean,
of course, that the problem does not exist. But in official quarters
it is simply not raised. . . . Moreover, the subject is taboo. To
tackle it would mean to expose not only myself but also the order
to which I belong to fierce and unfair criticism, and this would
hamper our important work in other fields. My colleagues and I
feel that it would be desirable if in your volume you would not
deal with the subject in our situation because our bishops would
be quite angry with the author and with *Concilium*."

Obviously not all refusals were based on these or similar
grounds. This holds primarily only for those countries already
referred to. Many reports dealing with a region that is geographically much too vast and too varied necessarily had to emphasize
certain points, and none of the authors would deny that these
reports are therefore to a certain extent "subjective". The difficulties mentioned above and to be referred to again in the Bibliographical Survey itself show not only that the Church has still
a great deal to learn about fairness within the Church in the

matter of free and businesslike discussion and about serious mutual consideration in this kind of questions, but also that the Church cannot have the necessary ability to start such a dialogue within when—in various ways—she is hampered in her freedom *from outside*. This is a useful hint for the right assessment of the discussion about celibacy: the issue itself and the discussion depend on an infinite number of theological, psychological, sociological, historical and political elements.

The Bibliographical Survey may help to make us critically aware of these manifold strands. This is a necessary preliminary for further discussion wherever it may lead.

THE DISCUSSION ON CELIBACY
IN ITALY, PORTUGAL AND SPAIN

Mario Cuminetti, Bergamo, Italy

I

THE GENERAL SITUATION

We can obtain a quick idea of the way the nations of Italy, Portugal and Spain approach the discussion on priestly celibacy by recalling that they depend, theologically speaking, a good deal on French—and, to a lesser extent, German—scholars. More recently, they have also been greatly influenced by the echoes of the discussions in the Netherlands and the writings of E. Schillebeeckx. With few exceptions—which, however, are increasing all the time—there are no original positions in theology. Consequently, the relations of magisterium and theology are conceived more on the order of respectful and quasi-passive expectation of the directives of the hierarchy. Instead of striving for reflection and discussions which anticipate themes, raise questions and explore even paths that are controversial, there is a preference for awaiting decisions and then explaining them in a rather a-critical fashion. This is all the more true when the problems are disputable and vital; hence, it holds good for the problem at issue here.

Therefore, we find ourselves often confronted by a rather negative fact: the open discussion of celibacy is left to newspapers and weeklies (with all the limits and prejudices common to this type of publishing), or to a few periodicals which, precisely on account of this, are looked upon with suspicion by the hierarchy. The official or semi-official periodicals are always lined up on the official positions. This was true even after the encyclical on priestly celibacy which allowed for positive discussion. And it is indicative that almost the totality of the clerical periodicals did not dedicate any, or scarcely any, commentaries to the document of Paul VI, limiting themselves to the polemic response to more shaded or more critical positions.[1]

II

THE POSITIONS

The reasons adduced in favor of retaining priestly celibacy are practically all those found in the encyclical. This holds for studies previous to the encyclical [2] as well as for commentaries published after it. From 1960 onward, an ever greater awareness of the

[1] In 1967 the Italian clerical reviews carried almost no articles on the subject. The Portuguese periodical *Lumen* limited itself to publishing the translation of Karl Rahner's letter on celibacy. In Spain, *Ilustracion del Clero* dedicated various pages to the subject, but of a rather polemical character: cf. the notes signed "Illustrator" (1967, pp. 665-70; 1968, pp. 304-14); B. Prada, *Roma ha hablado sobre el celibato,* 1967, pp. 268-85. A periodical which dedicated space to the subject in a moderate tone is *Incunable.* Among the commentaries on the encyclical we might cite: A. Leite, *O celibato sacerdotal* (Broteria, 1967), pp. 498-515; G. De Rosa, "Il celibato sacerdotale nel pensiero di Paulo VI," in *La Civiltà Cattolica* III (1967), pp. 209-22.

[2] Among a host of publications we might cite: J. C. Fernandez-Cid, J. Huergo, etc., *El celibato sacerdotal* (Salamanca, 1959); E. Balducci, *Perché i preti non si sposano* (Milan, 1962); C. de Villapadierna, *El celibato y la Biblia* (1961), pp. 3-12; G. de Rosa, "Il celibato sacerdotale," in *La Civilta Cattolica* II (1967), pp. 547-62; IV, pp. 422-39.

distinction between celibacy and priesthood can be observed as well as a minor insistence on the reason of the greater availability of the celibate priest.[3] Finally, even some of those who support the present practice of the Latin Church makes a distinction between the reasons for priestly celibacy and religious celibacy.[4]

More often than not there is a harsh tone toward anyone who places the present practice in discussion and toward priests who renounce it.[5] After the encyclical, the positions remain for the most part unchanged; however, there is a new emphasis that since the pope has spoken, discussion should come to an end.[6]

On the other hand, those who do not consider the problem terminated approach it from diverse points of view. I will mention them, beginning with a 1959 study by the Italian Dominican R. Spiazzi.[7] Citing the lack of priestly vocations and the difficul-

---

[3] Cf. Balducci, *op. cit.*, pp. 42, 131; T. Goffi, *L'integrazione affettiva del sacerdote* (Brescia, 1967), pp. 26-27.

[4] The priest is such not through a scientific study of perfection but through the sacramental exercise of the function of Christ (Balducci, *op. cit.*, pp. 42ff.). This theme is also developed—even if with different reasoning—by some who uphold the freedom of the priest as regards celibacy: A. Zarri, *Teologia del probabile* (Turin, 1967). See also the account by R. Martinez concerning a discussion that took place in the Accademia Alfonsiana in Rome ("El celibato eclesiasticos. Dialogo Professores-alumnos de la Acad. Alf. de Roma," in *Pentecostes* 10 (1966), pp. 54-65). However, it seems to me that the distinction must be made even sharper as is also shown by the students' conclusions after this "dialogue".

[5] We find expressions in the following vein: "demolishers of the faith and traditions", "subversive propaganda of the dissatisfied", marriage which "separates heart and life", "monopolistic" human love, etc. Cf. the aforementioned works of B. Prada, C. de Villapadierna, and G. De Rosa. See also: B. Lavaud, "Cause e rimedi alle attuali defezione della vita sacerdotale e religiosa," in *Rivista di ascetica e mistica* (1967), pp. 336-48. Furthermore, the reasons of the upholders of freedom of choice between marriage and celibacy are often presented in a gross and distorted manner. See J. J. Alvarez, "Errores modernos," in *El celibato sacerdotal*, pp. 81-113.

[6] "Roma loquta, causa finita," writers B. Prada, *op. cit.*, p. 268; "With full knowledge of the case, the Church has placed a firm period to the debate": G. De Rosa, *art. cit.*, p. 211; after this solemn pronouncement "discussions have no meaning at all, or merely a scandalous one": *L'Osservatore Romano*, Aug. 6, 1967.

[7] "Annotazione," in *Monitor ecclesiasticus* (1959), pp. 369-409. The section regarding the proposals on celibacy (pp. 387ff.) concludes with

ties presently encountered by priestly celibacy, the author proposed that the possibility should be studied of admitting married men not only to the diaconate but to the priesthood as well. In practice this meant an orientation toward a threefold type of clergy: (1) married, with ordinary functions of worship, (2) celibates, dependent on the diocesan bishop, and (3) celibates, dependent on the pope for more generalized and specialized tasks.

This proposal stirred up lively polemics, and some interpreted the speech given by John XXIII on January 27, 1960 to the Roman synod as being against such a proposal. As a matter of fact, P. Spiazzi subsequently published other articles to mitigate and clarify his position.[8]

III

THE POINTS UNDER DISCUSSION

This approach to the problem gave way—though without minimizing the idea of lack of priests—to more intrinsic considerations concerning the nature of the relationship between celibacy and priesthood.[9] The points most treated are: (1) the ever clearer distinction between celibacy and priesthood, (2) the acceptance of the reasons in favor of celibacy but insistence on the fact that they do not exclude objections,[10] and (3) the distinc-

---

the statement: "In something which is not essential according to the Gospel, it is necessary to proceed with intelligence and courage."

[8] "Santità di una legge," in *L'Osservatore Romano*, June 15, 1960. In this note which summarized a fuller study that appeared in *Monitor Ecclesiasticus* (1960: pp. 26-30), the Italian Dominican enlarged the problematic with respect to the first study. He no longer proposed the previous solution, although he did re-present the question concerning the dearth of vocations.

[9] See A. Zarri, *op. cit.;* P. Balestro, "Per un celibato positivo," in *Vita e Pensiero* 11 (1967), pp. 1172-83; R. Martinez, *op. cit.* See also the September and October issues of the periodical *Incunable* and the commentary on the encyclical by C. M. Beattle in *Questiones de vida cristiana* 31 (1967), pp. 110-20. In addition, there are many articles and publications which divulged the positions of the foreign scholars favorable to freedom of choice.

[10] These reflections are developed more fully by Balestro (*op. cit.*, p.

tion between opinion and the teaching of the Church, and between the opinion of the bishop of Rome and historical solution.

It seems to me that the real divergence lies in the second point in which the interlocutors have not yet clearly understood one another. There is indeed agreement that the charism of celibacy is not necessarily present in someone who feels called to the priesthood. There is also substantial agreement about the reasons adduced in favor of celibacy. However, this consensus does not result in a complete agreement because the point of departure is different. One side starts from considerations of a more personalistic character and terminates with freedom of choice; the other starts from "objective" considerations and terminates with a celibate priesthood.

Precisely because the points of departure are different, an authentic dialogue fails to be established. Those who favor retention of the present practice do not realize that the reasons they adduce—even if they are just—are not decisive in the eyes of their opponents who insist on the necessity of the charism of virginity which is not necessarily related to the priestly vocation. Hence, while they accept the reasons behind the celibate state, they note that if a person is not called to it, he cannot live it in such a manner; [11] he will live it in marriage, in the modality proper to that state.

The problem seems to be summarized best by González-Ruiz: "The problem of virginity and continence does not present itself as a value in itself, but in its relations toward the 'witnessing' or 'militant action' within the Church. Considered under this aspect, ecclesiastical celibacy is a problem which stems not from divine origin but belongs rather to the exclusive competence of

---

1172): "Contrary to other sectors in which an objection held to be valid cancels what is objected to, or the response to the objection cancels the objection itself, this does not seem to occur here; both are partly right, and the reasoning of one is not in a position to render the other wrong." The reasons for the choice of celibacy "are not uniquely definable for all" (p. 1183).

[11] Therefore, they do not regard the intervention of the pope as decisive; cf. Beattle, *op. cit.*; A. Zarri, *op. cit.*

the Church that must resolve it in every case according to the requirements of a particular existential situation." [12] Practically speaking, those who uphold the present practice fall more or less into the danger of making celibacy an "end in itself", minimizing the existential situation which remains decisive for the others.

IV
THE CONCEPT OF PRIESTHOOD

Conditioned by these two different points of view, the concepts of the sacred and the priesthood also enter into the discussion, although we have found them scarcely mentioned—especially the former. As far as the concept of the sacred is concerned, the discussion is still between something sacred, conceived as an end in itself with which the priesthood would be invested, and the concept of sacred as a relation.[13] Concerning the nature of the priesthood, there is a divergence between those who uphold a purely "functional" concept and those who regard it as insufficient.

Even De Rosa is agreed that if we give the priesthood a definition which is based solely on its functions, celibacy is "something superfluous", and it cannot be imposed.[14] But this is insufficient inasmuch as the priest is for this Jesuit also the man of God consecrated to love of Christ. And it is at this point that the discussion commences, insofar as the reply is made that this is a dimension common to all Christians. The diversity lies in the manner in which it is lived: in celibacy or in marriage; it is not obvious why the priest must necessarily live it in celibacy.

[12] J.-M. González-Ruiz, "Il celibato 'apostolico' secondo S. Paolo," in *C'e un domani per il prete?* (Milan, 1968).

[13] Balestro, *art. cit.,* p. 1181. Cf. M. Cuminetti, "La Chiesa nell'epoca della secolarizzazione," in *Testimonianze* 101 (1968).

[14] G. De Rosa, *art. cit.,* pp. 221-22. Others, however, uphold a "functional" definition of the priesthood but still demand celibacy insofar as "it is situated in the line of evangelical witnessing" and so is required by the function (cf. J. Daniélou, *L'Osservatore Romano,* June 6, 1968).

THE DISCUSSION ON CELIBACY IN THE UNITED STATES

Thomas Pucelik, Peoria, Illinois

"The controversy over the celibacy of the clergy has already reached a point of no return." This is the judgment of Dr. John Cogley, the well-known Catholic writer and theologian in the U.S., who was asked to contribute to a recent symposium published in the *St. Louis Review,* March 8, 1968. The editors of this top-ranking Catholic diocesan paper wished to begin a dialogue with their readers concerning the essentials of religion. Cogley chose to wrote about the Church and the future.

Admitting that very few, if any, have any idea of what is going to happen in the Church in the immediate future, he went on to point out what seemed to be the direction of sweeping change which is coming about in the Church in America. Concerning the clergy he wrote: "Establishing a married clergy will require serious adjustments in parochial and diocesan organization, but the changes will be made. Already is it clear that the Church will have no choice but to go along with the view expressed in one poll after another taken among the clergy themselves."

Statement of the American Bishops

The question that is being asked by clergy and laity alike is whether or not "changes will be made". In November, 1967 the bishops of the U.S., meeting in Washington, D.C., issued a statement which reaffirmed the value of celibacy and declared that it would be "irresponsible . . . to hold out any hope that this discipline will be changed. Such expectation is without foundation". From this it would seem that all official discussion concerning this controversial subject was closed off, even if the National Conference of Catholic Bishops did announce a detailed program for the study on the life and ministry of priests. But the discussion and concern of American priests about celibacy did not come to an end with this episcopal statement.

The Debate

Prior to this statement of the American bishops, there was another which was issued by the participants in the National Symposium on Clerical Celibacy, held September 6-8, 1967 on the campus of the University of Notre Dame. This statement said that the participants supported "the proposal that diocesan priests of the Latin rite be permitted the option of marrying or remaining celibate while exercising the active ministry of the Church".

The papers presented at this symposium, together with an article on "Clerical Marriages: Ante and Post Facta", have been collected and published in the book *Celibacy: The Necessary Option* (Herder and Herder, 1968). The editor, George H. Frein, has also written an introduction that gives a summary of the discussion and public debate which led up to the holding of the symposium on clerical celibacy. This covers a period from June 9, 1965 to October 19, 1967.

The opening of the debate on celibacy is located in the pages of the *National Catholic Reporter* with an article by "Sacerdos Occidentalis" entitled: "Should the Council Look at Celibacy?" But the article by Fr. James Kavanaugh, written under the pseudonym of Stephen Nash, was the first direct challenge to the law of celibacy which appeared in the secular press. His article in the *Saturday Evening Post* (March 12, 1966), "I Am a Priest, I Want to Marry", said something that had only been thought of but never before publicly expressed.

Kavanaugh's later book *A Modern Priest Looks at His Outdated Church* (Trident Press, 1967) became a best-seller and his ideas on the priesthood and celibacy, as well as many other problems of the Church, were read, and are being read, by thousands. He explained why he wrote the article for the *Post* and he attacked what was to him mere legalism, "a senseless law". He said that the priests accepted a way of life that they did not understand, and continued to embrace the laws of the Church because they were robbed of courage to "stand alone".

The Fichter Survey

But as this priest was expressing his feelings "alone", there were others who were joining together and organizing to bring about some action concerning the problem. Together with the editor of the *National Catholic Reporter* (NCR), Robert J. Hoyt, a group of priests arranged to have a survey taken to find out the attitudes of the American clergy concerning their priestly life. The results of this survey have been recently published in the book *America's Forgotten Priests—What They Are Saying* (Harper & Row, 1968), by Joseph H. Fichter, S.J. The original press release which appeared December 12, 1966 in the *NCR* received widespread attention. The Fichter survey showed that 62 percent of the more than 3,000 priests who responded (only non-pastors and non-monsignors were contacted) favored making the discipline of celibacy optional (while only 5 percent would unquestionably marry if given an option). Hardly a Catholic periodical has failed to review and to comment on this survey, though some, like *U.S. Catholic* (May, 1968), do not take any note of Chapter 8, "Married Clergy".

As the early reports of the Fichter survey indicated that there might be a majority of priests in the country favoring a change of legislation, the same priests who had instigated the survey called together others whom they thought might be interested in working for "optional celibacy". The National Association for Pastoral Renewal was then formed in November, 1966.

Even though it was rumored that the pope intended to issue an encyclical on celibacy, plans were made for NAPR to sponsor a public, interdisciplinary symposium on this question in the fall of 1967. Even *America* which had previously objected (July, 1965) to public discussion of celibacy editorialized (April, 1967): "The plan of the National Association for Pastoral Renewal is realistic and responsible . . . concrete and constructive , , . and it appears workable."

A Proposal for a Practical Solution?

The plan of NAPR ultimately was not only to conduct public discussion but also to make explicit a proposal made by Robert T. Francoeur in the pages of *Jubilee* (October, 1966) when he wrote: "They [far-sighted and apostolic bishops] might begin [to find a practical solution before we face a real crisis] by banding together in a very flexible group some of the talented and dedicated priests who have recently asked Rome for permission to marry and as a result have also been forced to accept being laicized. . . . The raw material is available for such a project." From the rather vague idea of "banding together" or "a project" came the explicit proposal of NAPR which called for the erection of a special ordinariate to guide and supervise the introduction of optional celibacy in the U.S. It was felt that the Apostolic Letter *Ecclesiae Sanctae* of October 24, 1966 (*AAS* 58: 760-761) provided the canonical basis when the Holy See announced the willingness to erect *praelaturae* for special apostolates.

"Optional Celibacy"

The Notre Dame Symposium was held and NAPR held its first public meeting, electing officers to work with the membership to attain the goal of "optional celibacy". The survey which Fichter had undertaken was expanded, and it was shown that at least 7,000 priests could be said to favor a change of legislation, while the new lay-edited paper *Twin Circle* has shown in its survey that some 90% of the pastors and monsignors interviewed opposed a change in the discipline of celibacy.

Criticism of the NAPR symposium was expressed in an *Ave Maria* editorial (September 23, 1967) which stated that "the option to marry will . . . find sympathetic hearing in the Church when its proper context is explained and when the underlying reasons why it is good for the Church become clear". This seems to be what has been developing. The "proper context" seems to be the perspective of the newly formed National Federation of

Priests' Councils which represents about 48,000 of the 60,000 priests in the U.S. It was reported that the delegates approved working directives for permanent committees which "range from study of specifically priestly problems, like optional celibacy . . . to broad problems affecting the whole Church, such as conscientious objection and lay and clerical participation in election of bishops" (NCR, May 29, 1968).

As to the question of why optional celibacy might be good for the Church or not, there is, of course, much debate. Bishop John J. Wright, in his article "The Vocation Crisis" (*Our Sunday Visitor,* March 10, 1968) spoke of a new harvest of vocations "on God's terms". He seemed to imply that this meant "by lifelong public witness of the counsels of poverty, chastity and obedience". Yet the American hierarchy has agreed to finance an indepth study of the priestly life which will include the question of celibacy. The editors of the *St. Louis Review* (April 19, 1968) wrote: "The willingness of the bishops to face pastoral questions is seen in their ongoing study of the life and ministry of priests. This is an area of grave concern in the Church. The bishops have gathered some of the finest experts in the country to assist them. The fact that Archbishop Dearden met with representatives of the NAPR in March 1968 and that the question of priestly celibacy will be included in the study shows a desire to face rather than to hide from touchy questions that affect the lives of Christians." This study is expected to take three years. Perhaps by then the problems of laicization and new structures (cf. J. H. Fichter, "Bishops Ought To Marry," *Commonweal,* May, 1968) for a "pluriform clergy" (Philip Sharper, *The Critic,* February, 1968) will have been solved, and it will have become clear what is for the good of the Church and the kingdom of God's love and peace.

THE DISCUSSION ON CELIBACY IN LATIN AMERICA

Manuel Edwards, SS.CC./Santiago, Chile

It cannot be said that there as yet exists in Latin America a public debate on priestly celibacy. There are many writings in private circulation on the subject and many translations from European or North American reviews, but there is very little original writing. And this is not because the subject lacks interest for the Church of Latin America. Everything that concerns the priest's style of life and image has a direct connection with the hope of vocations in a continent so desperately in need of them. This fact causes the subject to be approached mainly from the pastoral point of view, not that doctrinal or anthropological reflection is lacking.

The Value of Priestly Celibacy

Both before and after the encyclical of Paul VI, reflections and opinions concerning priestly celibacy appeared in certain important publications.

It is proper to indicate first of all the effort that has been made to draw out the full meaning of celibacy. To this group of writings belong the articles of Enrique E. Fabbri, "Celibacy and Sexuality" and "Celibacy and the Kingdom of Heaven",[1] and that of Fr. Manuel Ossa, S.J., "Love and Celibacy",[2] which, while primarily interested in the situation of the priest, provide a clear commentary on celibacy in general. Approaching the matter from the angle of history and theology, Urbano Zilles exalts the value of priestly celibacy in his article "Concerning Priestly Celibacy":[3] "Consecrated virginity is the visible sign that the Christian is capable of renouncing everything for love of Christ; the Church is free to fix on that form of life for her priests which seems to her most adapted to their salvific mission of service" (p.

[1] The review *Criterio* (Buenos Aires), March 9 and June 8, 1967.
[2] The review *Mensaje* (Santiago, Chile), December 1965.
[3] The review *Vozes* (Petropolis, Brazil), November 1966.

942). Hernán Larraín, S.J., approaches the subject from another angle in "Celibacy: The Psychological Point of View" [4] and brings out all the value contained in it at the same time as its complexity and the demands it makes in the matter of selection and formation of candidates. The spirituality of celibacy and its contribution to the state of matrimony in the Church is the subject chosen by Enrique Alvear, bishop of San Felipe (Chile).[5] Of particular interest is the article by Carlos Manuel de Céspedes, "Priesthood and the Situation in Cuba".[6] He writes: "The Church's demand of celibacy, about which there is, and should be, so much discussion, appears under the conditions of our life in the fullness of its significance. Priestly celibacy immeasurably enriches the witness of a priest's unconditional availability, speaking with an eloquence that our people understand perfectly. My opinion is that the canon law of celibacy should be revised and that the Eastern legislation is more evangelical in character; but, I emphasize, never did I esteem priestly celibacy so highly as I do now, after three years' ministry in Cuba."

It is logical to consider next the defense offered of the present canonical legislation. Fr. Salamón Rahim, S.J., in his book *Married Priests: Why Not?* [7] offers an extensive analysis and defense of Paul VI's encyclical and of the law of celibacy. A somewhat more temperate expression of the same point of view is given by Jorge Mojía, editor of the *Revista Criterio*; "It is perfectly understandable that the Church should demand of certain of her members that they should live without a wife. If by doing so she runs the risk of institutionalizing charismas, she would by not doing so run another, much greater, risk—that of not rising to the level, at least in principle, of the gifts which have been promised us." [8] Another defense of the present law is provided by Carmelo Giaquinta in his article "Priestly Celibacy Today",[9] in which he

---

[4] *Mensaje,* August 1966.
[5] The review *Teologia y Vida* (Santiago), January-March 1967.
[6] *Criterio,* October 13, 1966.
[7] An editorial in *Jus* (Mexico), 1968.
[8] *Criterio,* July 27, 1967.
[9] *Criterio,* June 9, 1966.

says: "For as long as the Church is able to provide for the needs of a faithful people with celibate priests, not only can she—but she does well to—assert that the priestly ministry should be entrusted only to celibates, as is the law in the Latin Church up to the present moment" (p. 425).

Abolition of the Law of Celibacy?

Some writers, however, have come out in a very different sense, in opposition both to the law of celibacy and to the above-mentioned encyclical. Fr. Napoleao da Costa, in his work "Bachelor Priests, Married Priests",[10] argues against this legislation; the facts of the situation, as much those of the priesthood as an institution as those of the present-day position in which priests find themselves, are his point of departure: "Can it be that celibacy is the only state of life compatible with the priesthood? When Christ chose his apostles, did he make celibacy an absolute condition?" (p. 20). "If it is true to say that celibacy is not essential to the priesthood, it is perfectly possible for the following situation to arise: a candidate may have a vocation to the priesthood, yet not have one for celibacy" (p. 39). A much cooler and very much more profound analysis is given by Dr. Paulo E. Andrede Ponte, in his article "Priestly Celibacy and the Law of Celibacy": [11] "What is desired by many serious and responsible Catholics is not the abolition of priestly celibacy but the abolition of the *law* which makes celibacy obligatory for priests" (p. 567). "Christian celibacy imposed by law is a contradiction in terms: a gift of God cannot be imposed by law" (p. 555). "Celibacy is being imposed by law on candidates for the priesthood instead of priesthood being granted by law only to those who have freely chosen the charism of celibacy" (p. 552). "The canonical law on celibacy, instead of 'upholding the charisma', casts into doubt its authenticity. To my mind an authentic celibacy is precisely what is compromised by the present canonical legislation" (p. 562). "Looking forward to a change

---

[10] *Belo Horizonte* (Brazil), 1965.
[11] *Revista Eclesiastica Brasileira,* September 1967.

in the law currently in force only intensifies in me the strength and love which give to my own celibacy security and happiness" (p. 566). "Could it not be argued, perhaps, that this preoccupation with maintaining the law of celibacy reveals a fear that without the law the number of celibate priests will diminish notably? Would it not be better to leave it to the Lord to raise up vocations alike to the priesthood and to celibacy, without referring in either case to a kind of juridical pressure?" (p. 567).

The Future of the Latin American Church and Celibacy

Finally, the opinion is being expressed in many countries that, while the present law might be maintained, the priesthood could nonetheless be conferred on married persons. The bishop of Lins (Brazil), Pedro Paulo Koop, in the speech he was unable to make before the Council and therefore published subsequently,[12] said: "Let nothing be changed in the present order of things. Only let there be introduced some other pastoral instrument, capable of providing a radical remedy to our lamentable religious situation, both for today and for the near future. Let the bishops be under no illusion! The destiny of the Latin American Church is at stake! A choice is forced upon us: either to multiply without delay the number of priests, chosen from among either bachelors or the married, or to witness the wretched eclipse of the Church in Latin America" (p. 911). Elías Andreos, exarch of the Catholic Melkite community of Buenos Aires, writes in the same sense: [13] "We are confronted by two imperatives, the first of the divine order and the second of the ecclesiastical. The first is that of the right of the People of God to receive that spiritual ministration demanded by its eternal salvation. The second is that of ecclesiastical law which, by its demands, does not allow the fulfillment in the concrete and practical order of that first divine imperative. We are not trying to tone down, still less to derogate from, a law which is not beyond the moral capacities of man if he uses supernatural

[12] *Vozes,* November 1966.
[13] *Criterio,* March 9, 1967.

means; our purpose is rather to synthesize it with another law which will allow us to find a viable and practical solution to an acute problem which will otherwise grow day by day more complex and more grave" (p. 151).

The pastoral synod of the Church of Santiago (Chile) [14] expressed itself in the following terms: "The synod wishes, in continuity both with Vatican Council II and with the encyclical, to reaffirm the especial value attaching to the charism of celibacy as a sign of that which the priest proclaims in his words and realizes by his priestly ministry. The necessity is manifest of consecrating to the diaconate and, eventually, to the priesthood, those men, whether bachelors or married, whom the Spirit raises up in our communities" (p. 138). The "Charter of the Two Hundred" [15] states this opinion in precise terms that go to the root of the matter and put it in its true context: "When will Chile come to its maturity as the People of God? Why should not access to the priesthood be given to married men, coming from the same local communities, as in the early Church? It is obvious that one would be dealing with married men for the simple reason that to reach the standing of a leader is not usual at the age of twenty. The leaders that arise in human communities come into the open when they reach adult life and are already married. Why do we make an essential obstacle out of something which is not one and which prevents us from providing a solution to so grave a problem" (p. 7). "The criterion of Paul VI (n. 38 of the encyclical) is illuminating: the historical situation conditions in every respect the way in which the Holy Spirt acts. It could also be the case that now, in new historical situations and under new anthropological conditions, the Holy Spirit should adapt his inspiration to them. We ask ourselves: Could this not be the case for Latin America?"(p. 9).

To what extent are these reflections and opinions shared by the clergy and the churches of the various Latin American countries? It is very hard to say, since there exists no serious and wide-

14 Post-conciliar Archdiocesan Commission, September 1967.
15 Letter of 219 foreign priests to the bishops of Chile, August 1967.

ranging survey of opinion on this point. However, one thing is certain: in every country there is reflection and discussion on this theme, even though little may be written. The ordination of married men is considered indispensable for the care of grass-roots communities, given the fact that foreign priests cannot provide an adequate solution. New light is shed on the value attaching to the charism of celibacy. Both defenders of the present law and those who desire its suppression rest their most powerful arguments precisely on this valuation of the charism or on pastoral motives. And there is no doubt that what is fundamental for Latin America is this last aspect, given the fact that its Church is the most poverty-stricken in priests in the whole world. In Australia there is one priest for 696 Catholics, in North America one for 732, in Europe one for 904, in Asia one for 1,661, and in Africa one for 1,754; in Latin America there is one priest for 4,985.[16]

The Discussion on Celibacy in Africa

Daniel Pasu-Pasu, S.J., Kinshasa-Kalina, Congo

The State of the Question

Both before and during Vatican Council II a certain section of the press organized a campaign in favor of a married priesthood in the Latin Church. One of the principal arguments urged in favor of this was the progressive dwindling of vocations, particularly in mission countries which are, for the most part, underdeveloped. This opinion won a hearing and a certain sympathy in a significant number of priests. It may be that this attitude was dictated primarily by Christian charity for those countries in which Christianity has not yet been definitively established. But there are good grounds for a suspicion of insincerity when fac-

[16] Cf. "Latin America and Its Priests," in *Pro Mundi Vita* 22, 1968.

tion, extremism and public disobedience are the outcome. After all, have we not seen certain European priests, either in groups or individually, abandoning their diocese to marry, this allegedly in order to compel the Church to make up her mind on this problem? Is that the way to increase vocations in mission countries?

African priests find it extremely distasteful when certain Western theologians make use of their situation, often imperfectly understood, to justify their own theories or preoccupations. To my mind it is obvious that superficial discussion in the press concerning a question of such importance renders impossible the delicacy of treatment required by the subject and intensifies doubt in the mind of those priests who may be wavering or weak. It goes without saying that Congolese priests have welcomed the debate on ecclesiastical celibacy and followed it with interest. They had not the slightest intention either of refusing to join in or of pressing for the immediate and unreflecting implementation in their own country of whatever conclusions it may come to. But they have wanted to determine the boundaries of the discussion and its doctrinal implications.

It is no accident that the value of ecclesiastical celibacy should have been called into doubt at the same time as the Church was deepening her understanding of the theology of marriage and the lay apostolate. The dignity and beauty of conjugal love on the one hand and the effectiveness in certain situations of lay apostles could suggest and indeed have suggested that the presence of celibate priests within the Church was of no value for her. But in every university there exist many faculties. No student can choose them all simultaneously. The human situation unceasingly compels us to make choices. If a man chooses a given course of studies that corresponds to his personal aspirations, that is no sort of indication that he despises the other courses he did not choose. The existence of every single university faculty remains a necessity for the life of the nation, taken as a whole. I see no reason why the existence of celibate priests should be any sort of obstacle to the lay apostolate! There are mansions enough in the house of the Father.

Clerical marriage is not, to the mind of most Congolese priests, the key to the conversion of Africa, though they might concede that competent authority should carefully examine those particular cases, particularly with isolated tribes or villages, when there is a married man of known worth, approved formation and public repute whose ordination would be of service to the whole community.

The Contemporary Implications of Celibacy

To be honest, any attempt to come to objective and defensible conclusions on ecclesiastical celibacy that apply to the African clergy as a whole seems to me merely pretentious. Such conclusions would need for their support a series of sociological inquiries in every African country with any sort of clerical structure. To the best of my knowledge, there has been as yet no serious study whatever on this question. What we are giving here as our opinion is grounded on the general impression gained from conversations and meetings with Congolese priests. I will mention particularly the provincial consultations which prepared the ground for the report made to the 1967 conference of the Congolese bishops.

Even if no scientific study has been made of the fact, there is no doubt that the Latin Church has had in the course of her history, and still has today, weaknesses in her clergy. In all countries, even those once forming part of what was called "Christendom", a certain percentage of priests abandon their ministry; of this percentage various estimates are made, ranging between 5% and 30%. Every religiously developed country has a priestly elite, greater or lesser in number, which creates and upholds the reputation of the national clergy. We admit that the African socio-psychological attitude to fertility and the transmission of life can make the observance of chastity harder and more demanding.

We are arguing, of course, on the socio-psychological level

alone, and on this level, to judge by appearances, one might think that sex problems are intensified for young people today by the increasing prevalence of promiscuity and indecent fashions. This is the psycho-sociological context within which young people today have to make their option for ecclesiastical celibacy, and they take with them the difficulties inherent in their outlook and formation. It is not by chance that modern science has been researching ever more deeply into psychology with a view either to restoring equilibrium in the psyche of those whose milieux have destroyed it or to give peace to the troubled consciences of men living in objectively false situations.

Priests of Africa and the Present Upheaval

Every structure in the world is being shaken, and the effect of this has been felt as much by Congolese priests as by all others. They speak the language of their own age and make their own its ideas and forms of life. Some have failed in their mission of correcting and purifying the shortcomings of the People of God. This crisis of fidelity to consecrate celibacy has been the occasion for certain Western thinkers to see in this a situation peculiar to Africa. They have not hesitated to imply that the salvation of the African Church lay in the marriage of priests.

Without prejudice or partisan feeling, I would simply like to offer some facts for consideration. Is it known in the West that in the Congo certain religious situations demanded of officeholders that they abstain, at least for a time, from any use of marriage? That is why office was conferred normally on men of mature age. Is it known that formerly no warrior could approach a woman for the duration of hostilities, and this under pain of death? Is it known that on the eve of a great hunting or fishing expedition the entire village or tribe would abstain from any use of marriage? So also would a man on the eve of offering sacrifice.

All these things in African tradition are so many foreshadowings of what was to come. These few examples, to which many others could be added, show clearly that pre-Christian African society was not totally devoid of any notion of a continence consecrated by a religious ideal, as certain students of Africa seem to suggest. In our age there is a tendency to confuse fertility and sexuality. The impression is created that every manifestation of life-giving energy is necessarily sexual—a view which, taken to its logical conclusion, would be the absolute negation of the Christian religion whose entire sense lies in the gift of life: "Ego sum vita, via et veritas."

This being the case for the Congo and Africa, I would like to ask a fundamental question of universal contemporary validity. Will it from now on be possible for mankind to establish objective criteria in the field of education when in all others it has chosen unceasing change as the very principle of all development? The socio-cultural milieu is imbued with this evolutionary mentality; will it retain any capacity for assimilating those unchanging criteria and rules of action that are needed to guarantee the moral formation of future generations? What makes the problem even graver is that each new generation feels itself not simply different from the one before it but a stranger to it, even an enemy.

When one surveys the present situation of cultural breakdown out of which man is striving to produce a universal humanism, one is forced to confess that there is no immediate solution in sight. On the other hand, the African clergy is inevitably caught up in the interplay of world forces. Its problems in the field of ecclesiastical celibacy will not be peculiar to it, but common to the universal Church. After all, a world which has for its existential principles unceasing change and the instability of every received doctrine is no longer intelligible within a stable structure of traditional moral law. Stability is becoming an anachronism. Moreover, for us Christians, consecrated celibacy is a special vocation from God—that is, a grace. Any attempt to reduce it to mere considerations of psychotherapy or to explain it uniquely in terms of the principles of psychoanalysis seems to us a misunderstanding of its true character. From such a naturalistic standpoint the vocation to celibacy appears an enigma, an arbitrary violation of what is evidently right.

The problem of ecclesiastical celibacy takes its origin in the present state of doubt concerning the comparative value of Christian marriage and the apostolic zeal of committed laymen. A defective theology of ecclesiastical celibacy can lead to a corrosive anxiety and even to a refusal of vocation. Were we not by nature ordered to marriage, our celibacy would lose by that same token all its value as a "special" vocation, and we priests would become a caste composed of the generous but abnormal! The discovery of the world of woman can lead consecrated but uncertain hearts to a ruinous nostalgia and every sort of dubious situation.

The natural desire to see oneself perpetuated in one's posterity is not peculiar to Africa. The major portion of the globe is not populated by Africans! Cardinal Léger, in his letter on "Ecclesiastical Celibacy" (*Orientations Pastorales* 111 [1967], p. 106), said: "Love of the Church is not a poor reflection of or substitution for the love of husband and wife. It is the norm that can inspire every love with fervor, delicacy and the desire of highest good for the other. The priest and the religious, man or woman, are never alone, since they have chosen to give their love to one who is perfect, real, present in all places and faithful at all times."

Conclusion: There Is No African Solution

We all know what St. Paul says about celibacy in 1 Corinthians 7, 32-33. It seems clear enough that in the plan of God ecclesiastical celibacy, which is a vocation of service, is not a call that goes counter to the work of God but rather one that forms an integral part of it. A harmony is founded on the diversity of the elements that make up the whole, not on their uniformity. The existence of so many species of living creatures is a manifestation of God's power and generosity. If the Church needed married priests in Africa, she could have ordained them as such in response to the multifarious needs of the continent, and not under pressure from the rebellion of nature against the demands of celibacy.

THE DISCUSSION ON CELIBACY IN ENGLAND AND IRELAND

Enda McDonagh, Maynooth, Ireland

At the time of writing (July 1968) the discussion in these countries has not taken on the intensity and urgency associated with it elsewhere. It cannot compare, for instance, with the intensity and urgency of the "contraception" debate in these countries. The absence of any very noticeable reaction to the papal encyclical on celibacy (June 1967) is one obvious indication of this,[1] and one looks in vain for publications or movements actively campaigning for or against priestly celibacy. Much of the more urgent writing appearing is translated from German, French or Dutch, or taken from the United States, and will not be considered here.

Part of the reason for the comparative quiet is the relative sufficiency of priests and vocations which these countries have recently enjoyed. And although there are no official or even well-documented figures for defections from the priesthood in order to marry, it was commonly and reasonably believed that up to recently there were relatively very few.[2]

The Meaning of Celibacy

The most encouraging feature of the discussion has been the many positive attempts to understand the role of celibacy in the life and witness of the Christian Church. The understanding has

[1] Cf. *The Tablet* (London), July 1967; The *Catholic Herald*, June 30, 1967.

[2] In a report from London in *The National Catholic Reporter* (Kansas City), June 12, 1968, Kevin Mayhew suggests that the number may have risen quite considerably in England in 1967 and still more rapidly in the early part of 1968. However, beyond personal impressions, no exact knowledge is available. This makes public discussion of the problem of defection somewhat unreal. It is clear that those who leave have not considered themselves called to witness publicly against association of priesthood and celibacy. The English theologian Charles Davis, who rejected the Church and then married, later affirmed his belief in the value of celibacy and did not wish to be interpreted as making a gesture against a celibate clergy. Cf. A. Davis, *A Question of Conscience* (London, 1967), pp. 30ff.

been characterized at all levels by the conviction that Christian marriage and Christian celibacy belong together.

The association of marriage and celibacy provides the key to understanding St. Paul's teaching, according to biblical scholar Lionel Swain.[3] For him, 1 Corinthians 7 "is clearly a literary unit comprising three main sections: vv 1-16, concerning the married, or those who have been married; vv 17-24, an exhortation to all to remain in the state in which they have been called; vv 25-38, concerning virgins."[4] In the section on marriage Paul expresses his preference for celibacy; in the section on celibacy he emphasizes the goodness of marriage. His essential message is that "each person should remain in the state in which he was called".[5] His preference for celibacy refers "not to a state to be acquired, but to a condition in which one is called",[6] and is based on the more explicit witness to the resurrection which celibacy involves, and by which it completes marriage.

The complementarity of marriage and celibacy is given explicit theological treatment by the Maynooth theologians Denis O'Callaghan and Enda McDonagh.[7] Marriage and celibacy emphasize and incorporate differing aspects of the one Christian reality, the saving event of Jesus Christ in its already achieved and yet incomplete state. Marriage reflects more explicitly the already achieved; it bears witness to the fullness and saving effect of the incarnation whereby humanity in all its dimensions and above all human love became the bearer of the divine in the world. Celibacy is a forceful reminder of the yet to be. The consummation is not yet. The radical renunciation of the human fulfillment of marriage, in the full understanding of its value, human and Christian, and for the sake of the kingdom of God, expresses more eloquently than any words could, the pilgrim on-the-way-to-

---

[3] L. Swain "Paul on Celibacy," in *The Clergy Review*, October 1966, p. 785.

[4] *Ibid.*, p. 786.

[5] *Ibid.*, p. 786.

[6] *Ibid.*, p. 787.

[7] D. O'Callaghan, "Marriage and Celibacy," in *Truth and Life* (Dublin, 1968), pp. 164ff. Cf. E. McDonagh, "Marriage and Virginity," in *The Meaning of Christian Marriage* (Dublin, 1963), pp. 167ff.; *idem*, "Christian Marriage in an Ecumenical Context," in *The Furrow* XIX/1 (Maynooth, January 1968), pp. 3ff.

perfection condition in which men must live here on earth. The apparent self-sufficiency of marriage and of its human loving needs this reminder, just as celibacy could be misunderstood as flight from the world, rejection of the created and redeemed value of sex, if it were not balanced by an understanding and acceptance of marriage.

At the more practical and existential level, the complementarity has been developed by Ferghal O'Connor, O.P.,[8] Rosemary Haughton [9] and Marie Arnall.[10] Their treatment of the relationship between the two at the level of human experience and in the life of the Church should enable married and celibate Christians to bear one another's burdens in going forward to their common goal. As Mrs. Haughton points out: "The nearer to Christ any Christian comes, the less is there any important difference in his 'spirituality', as between married and celibate." [11] Yet it is at the level of daily painful involvement for both that their Christian need of each other becomes most obvious.

Celibacy and the Ministry

In such a context the relationship of celibacy to the ministry might expect calm and fruitful consideration. Yet very little "native" literature has appeared. What has appeared has been mostly in the form of letters reacting to articles or reports emanating from the mainland of Europe or America. In criticism of the views of E. Schillebeeckx, O.P., reported in *Herder Correspondence,*[12] a number of letters [13] took issue with his emphasis on the close association ("intimate tendency rather than strict demand" [14]) between priesthood and celibacy. The criticism

[8] F. O'Connor, "Sexuality, Chastity and Celibacy," in *Celibacy and Virginity* (Dublin, 1968), pp. 25ff.

[9] R. Haughton, Introduction to *Celibacy and Virginity, op. cit.;* "Marriage and Virginity," in *Doctrine and Life* XVII/11 (Dublin, November 1967), pp. 587ff.

[10] M. Arnall, "Some of Us Are Celibates," in *Bulletin of the Catholic Marriage Advisory Council* 8/2, 1968.

[11] "Marriage and Virginity," *art. cit.,* p. 590.

[12] *Herder Correspondence,* I/9-10 (September-October 1964), pp. 266ff.

[13] *Herder Correspondence,* II/3 (March 1965), p. 94; II/6 (June 1965), p. 190; III/6 (June 1965), p. 189; III/8 (August 1965), p. 251.

[14] E. Taylor, "Christian Celibacy," in *The Furrow* XVI/8 (August 1965), pp. 484ff.

stressed the non-biblical character of the present discipline, the preservation of the "apostolic tradition" in Eastern Churches, the dubious origins of the thinking on sex and marriage which led to its introduction, the recovery of a fuller theology of marriage, the limitation on the freedom of the priest, especially in light of the distinction of the callings, and the practical disadvantages of the present ruling.[15]

Similar criticisms were repeated in a correspondence in *The Furrow*. The writer who was criticized had been dealing with the meaning and value of celibacy in itself, not defending its connection with the ministry. In reply he stated that this question needs open discussion: "It is my opinion that, because of the shortage of priests and the extreme difficulty of practicing celibacy under the peculiar stresses of modern times, in certain places, within certain limits and under certain conditions, the priesthood should be conferred on exemplary married men." [16]

The shortage of priests in the situation of modern Africa has been the basis of a very powerful plea by English missionary theologian Adrian Hastings for the gradual introduction of some married clergy, by ordaining catechists to the restored married diaconate and some of these later to the priesthood: [17] "The essential starting point for a sound line of thought is that a community which can provide baptized men must also, in a few years at the most, be able to provide a sufficient number of ordained men to minister to them. If this does not happen, it is because we are trying to impose a pattern of ministry worked out in different circumstances in such a way as to stifle the life of the young Church." [18]

In an editorial in the *Clergy Review*,[19] Michael Richards takes as his point of departure the ecumenical dialogue and the need to provide for a married clergy in the Western Church.

---

[15] E. McDermott, *The Furrow* XVI/10 (October 1965), pp. 634ff.; B. Martin, *loc. cit.*, pp. 637f.

[16] E. Taylor, *The Furrow* XVI/11 (November 1965), pp. 706ff.

[17] A. Hastings, *Church and Mission in Modern Africa* (London-New York, 1967); cf. *Herder Correspondence* V/3 (March 1968), pp. 70ff.

[18] A. Hastings, *op. cit.*

[19] "Month by Month," in *The Clergy Review* LIII/5 (May 1968), pp. 329ff.

The only extensive analysis of the present association of celibacy and ministry comes from Denis O'Callaghan.[20] He is, of course, aware that one cannot go beyond the argument from suitability as it was expressed in the encyclical and elaborated by a number of continental theologians—Rahner, Schillebeeckx and Auer—whose views have been recently published in English. And one of the great difficulties of all arguments *ex convenientia* is their inconclusiveness. The undoubtedly persuasive arguments from the christological, apostolic or eschatological role of the priest can be balanced by other "convenient" arguments. For a prudent pastoral ruling, which is all that the present discipline or any new one could claim to be, the arguments must necessarily be *ex convenientia*. But the *convenientia* must take account of the needs of the Church of a particular time and place and not just of theological parallels. And it remains within the right of the Church, as these authors say, to confine her calling of ministers to those with the special call of celibacy, if that seems the best solution in the circumstances.

Some Practical Considerations

Some of the most useful writing on this subject has been concerned with such practical issues as the choice and preparation of candidates and the living of priestly celibacy. Many of the present difficulties and the discussion they provoke come from inadequate selection procedure, defective preparation, and an unreal attitude to the living of celibacy.

The Irish psychologists [21] offer important help in selecting and training candidates according to the intention of the pope's plea in his recent encyclical. A number of authors also plead for a more human—i.e., loving—understanding and living of the celibate way, which must include the love of friendship both with people of one's own and of the other sex.[22] The presentation of

[20] *Loc. cit.*, pp. 178ff.

[21] E. Doherty, "Psychological Factors in the Priest's Vocation," in *Doctrine and Life* XVII/9 (September 1967), pp. 471ff.; F. Ford, "Personal Identity and Religious Commitment," *loc. cit.*, pp. 509ff.

[22] O'Connor, *op. cit.;* Arnall, *op. cit.;* Haughton, *op. cit.*

chastity in marriage and celibacy as something which must grow, and its understanding as "the measure of our capacity to love as men and women" [23] (celibate and married), will have a liberating effect on many Christians. To see the celibate as called to be a "model and master in the whole field of personal relationships" is to stress his true vocation precisely in the area of sexuality.[24]

The absence of any intense or emotional debate about the value of celibacy and its association with the priesthood robs excitement from any report from these islands. Yet in the growing appreciation of celibacy as a necessary complement of Christian marriage, and in attention given to the fuller living of it, recent British and Irish writing has made important progress and may be better equipped to handle such a debate if and when it arises.

THE DISCUSSION ON CELIBACY IN FRANCE,
GERMANY AND THE NETHERLANDS

Friedrich Wulf, S.J., Munich, W. Germany

In the countries of central and western Europe the celibacy debate hinges on more or less the same basic questions. If differences exist at all, then it is mostly in the vigor with which the discussion is pursued as people express their attitude to the Latin Church's *law* of celibacy. The debate is most heated in the Netherlands, and it would seem that Germany comes next, with France taking up the rear. There might well be some connection (at least as far as I can tell from the available literature) between the state of the debate in France and a greater consciousness in that country of the spiritual significance of celibacy than is to be found in either Germany or the Netherlands.

[23] O'Connor, *op. cit.*, p. 33.
[24] *Ibid.*, p. 44.

I

THE STARTING POINT

All are agreed that the present celibacy crisis is without parallel since Trent succeeded in making it obligatory. It is a crisis that has been building up for several years now, though only since Vatican Council II has it been conducted in public. Its causes are deep-seated, though the most fundamental of them are to be sought in the priest's inability to maintain his former social position in a world that has become increasingly secularized. It was for this reason that even the Council was unable to settle the matter. It made the mistake, so it is said, of seeing celibacy as an isolated problem of a predominantly theological and spiritual nature, and of course the public discussion that many people believed should take place at the time of the Council was never allowed. This is where the criticism begins. It is said that the official Church regards the celibacy question as taboo, as something one should not discuss in public, and, the argument goes on, this attitude must be set aside if the present crisis, with the resultant loss of confidence in ecclesiastical authority, is to be resolved. This situation of conflict explains the fact that, leaving aside the commentaries on the two conciliar decrees (*Decree on Priestly Training* and *Decree on the Ministry and Life of Priests*), very little notice has been taken of what the Council had to say about celibacy. In more polemical literature, mention of the conciliar treatment of the celibacy question has centered mainly and frequently on episcopal interventions whose object was either to push the discussion into the limelight or at least to make a few necessary points on behalf of those who recognized a real problem; or reference has been made to n. 16 of the *Decree on the Ministry and Life of Priests* (*Presbyterorum Ordinis*) where it is stated that celibacy "is not demanded by the very nature of the priesthood".

Moving further on, it is recognized that Pope Paul's encyclical on celibacy did even less to settle the arguments, even though it examined in detail many of the current objections to obligatory celibacy. Indeed, it can be said that this encyclical merely added fuel to the fire. Even its well-wishers had to observe that its very language and tone showed a misunderstanding of contemporary man. Others were prepared to overlook that, being more concerned by an insufficiently differentiated and unduly mystical identification between the priest and Christ which ran the risk of once again distancing priest from people. Still others commented that from the standpoint of hardheaded exegesis the many scriptural quotations were worthless, that the anthropological aspect of the problem was inadequately answered, that those priests who found it necessary to resign their ministry on account of difficulties with this problem were too readily faced with moral censure, and that the type of "compassion" shown to them by the Church looked too much like self-righteousness. Let it be added, however, that whereas the encyclical had an unfavorable reception, not many commentators stressed what was new and valuable in it.

II
THE HISTORY OF CELIBACY

Understandably the history of celibacy plays an important part in the discussion. History after all ought to show whether celibacy—particularly obligatory celibacy—owes its origin to Christian, pre-Christian or even non-Christian motives. Judgment on this point is by no means unanimous, which is hardly surprising since the history of this issue is extremely complex, influenced as it has been by a variety of attitudes and circumstances. "Historically the Church has handled the matter of *lex continentiae* with considerable discretion," writes L. Hödl ("Die lex continentiae," in *Zeitschr. für kath. Theologie* 83 [1961], p. 335). "This combination of prudence and steadfastness, of understanding and concern," he goes on to say "is still noticeable, and worth noting today." Hans Küng, on the other hand, takes a different view: "The Church will know no peace until the candidate for the priesthood is permitted to decide for himself whether or not he wishes to marry. This is how it was in the beginning, and peace will not return until an ecclesiastical law introduced in very problematic circumstances is once and for all annulled." There are others who go a lot further, presenting the law of celibacy as though its development were a chapter of errors, abuse of authority, and unpleasant footwork on the part of a domineering Roman institution.

Somewhere between these views are those whose attempts to see both sides of the picture lead them to the conclusion that "the decisive motive behind the development of priestly celibacy does in fact seem to be its biblical origin" (B. Kotting) and that in any event the reasons for maintaining the law have been increasingly Christianized as time has gone by (Schillebeeckx). This latter attitude is in tune with contemporary attempts in the Council and elsewhere to establish the basis and justification of celibacy and obligatory celibacy, for the reasons put forward in these arguments are adduced not "from outside" but exclusively from biblically based criteria that then lead on to what is acceptable to theology and appropriate to the office.

III
THE ROOT QUESTION

The root question is that of the admissibility of a law that obliges all priests of the Latin rite to make a binding connection between office and charism. How can the Church, the question goes, exclude office from marriage if the former does not itself demand it—as history shows and as the Council has recently stressed—and given that man's right to the latter is inalienable? To put the question the other way round: How can the Church impose by law on all who feel called to the priesthood a gift of grace "which the Father gives to some men" (*Constitution on the Church*, n. 42, with reference to Mt. 19, 11)? Does it make any sense at all to attempt to regulate and institutionalize by man-made law a Christian enthusiasm that is subject only to the "law" of gratuitously imparted grace? As far as I can see, this question is recognized to be a genuine question, and therefore also as a difficulty insofar as the charismatic basis of celibacy is nowadays stressed with increasing earnestness.

What answer do celibacy's defenders offer? First, it is maintained that the Church obliges nobody to accept celibacy. On the contrary, it only admits those to the priesthood to whom the charism of celibacy has been given and who therefore accept the charism in total freedom. If those of this persuasion dig deeper for their answers, it is maintained that the unmarried state "embraced on behalf of the kingdom of heaven" is fully in keeping with the "holy service of the Gospel" that the priestly office represents (Rom. 15, 16; cf. Mk. 10, 29), and that there is nothing exceptional in the fact that the man who is called to the office is given the charism of celibacy (cf. *Decree on the Ministry and Life of Priests,* n. 16: "It [the Council] trusts in the Spirit that the gift of celibacy, which so befits the priesthood of the New Testament, will be generously bestowed by the Father, as long as those who share in Christ's priesthood through the sacrament of orders, and indeed the whole Church, humbly and earnestly pray for it") if he is merely acceding to the charismatic basis of the office that (at least in its fullest expression) requires total dedication to Christ. People of this opinion go on to say that too many people have a false understanding of charisms, and that they talk as though these were gifts imparted once and for all, almost tangible things (for example, J. Wuermeling), whereas in fact each charism has its own history, a history that could be a courageous leap of faith onto uncertain ground.

Opponents of obligatory celibacy are not satisfied by this response. They argue, for instance, that the candidate for the priesthood frequently does not have the freedom claimed for him by the Church because he cannot foresee his future development and is therefore not in a position to know if he is suited to a celibate way of life; not a few, therefore, would simply regard celibacy as something that went with the job, only to discover later, perhaps, that they had chosen the wrong job.

Recognizing a degree of validity in these objections, the supporters of celibacy would like to see the freedom of candidates in this respect more thoroughly protected; they are looking for ways to achieve this goal (instruction on marriage, tests [e.g., work done in female company], postponement of ordination age), and are urging the case for easing a man's resignation from office, without defamation, if his situation is seen to require it.

IV

THE REASONS FOR THE CELIBACY CRISIS

Expert opinion believes that the reasons for the present celibacy crisis are inseparable from the changes brought about by world and society which have affected not only the priest's position but also his understanding of his role. The crisis is also associated with changes in the sphere of anthropology, sociology and theology. These changes are further ascribed to uncertainty of faith, a characteristic nowadays of many priests and of Christians generally.

In recent decades anthropology has introduced us to a deeper awareness of physical and sexual processes and of how inextricably bound up these are with the process of maturation. This has led the Church to adopt a new and more open attitude to both the body and sex, and above all to a revaluation of marriage which has for the first time enabled a comprehensive theology of marriage to emerge. As a direct consequence this has led to a fresh evaluation of virginity, which is now regarded as relative to the value of marriage. It was not possible for priestly celibacy to remain unaffected by all this rethinking. Wherever anthropologists, psychologists and doctors have joined in the celibacy discussion—those, that is, who have learned something about the type of difficulties many priests have on account of celibacy—they have, without exception in the literature I have examined, declared themselves in favor of permitting the candidate for the priesthood a free choice in the matter of marriage or celibacy. Their arguments are now being taken up by non-experts, including priests, but often they are repeated with such heavy emotional overtones that, in spite of the protestation that they have no wish to cast doubt on the value of virginity and its realization in the priesthood, one has the impression that the charism of celibacy is found only very exceptionally and should not be taken as normative.

As regards change of a sociological nature, the priest has lost his position in society, for it is now a society that of itself has none to offer him. He no longer knows what use he is (cf. Maurice Bellet). In the consequent vacuum, celibacy seems to be of questionable worth. Many authors are therefore arguing (for instance, Marc Oraison in *Le Monde* and P. Picard) that the celibacy question is in fact a secondary one. The celibacy crisis, they feel, is the symptom of a more fundamental crisis: the crisis of ministry in a secularized world. They find evidence for this in the parallel crisis that the Protestant Church is undergoing. Indispensable though it is to grapple with the problem by seeking out theological and spiritual causes and factors, this should not be the primary approach. It is more important, these writers conclude, to help the priest to recover his place in world and society.

Finally, concerning the theological presentation of the priestly ministry, it is important that the emphasis be not on ordination that raises him above others, but on his ministry of service to others. This is the point at which many people ask: How can the priest strengthen his position as a man among his fellow men, and what form should his ministry take if it is to be possible for him to live a celibate life, in spite of the loss of his special position and his consequent social segregation? To the same end, it is also asked what form the worshiping community should take? In what way can it help its priests to maintain a celibate way of life? This brings us to the last question.

V

WHAT OF THE FUTURE?

There can be no doubt that the trend is toward the removal of obligatory celibacy. This demand is often made in such a biased (from the point of view of marriage) and radical way that the indispensable role of celibacy in the Church is very largely lost sight of. There are therefore an increasing number of people anxious to warn of the sharp disappointment that will be experienced by those who think that once priests are permitted to choose as they please, the question of the role of the priesthood in the modern world will have been solved. It is becoming increasingly clear that the celibacy question cannot be examined in isolation—which, as we have seen, is the mistake the encyclical made—especially if one hopes to preserve the celibacy of the secular priesthood. It is important, many are saying, to change the structures, to adapt them to the actual situation: education, priestly life (Oraison), the parish and, above all, the ministry itself. There is no good reason why certain functions should not be extracted from the scope of the priestly ministry as we have known it so far, and handed over to married men, either sacramentally or simply by the acceptance of a mandate from a bishop. In this connection the recurrent suggestion is that the office of president (*Vorsteheraint*) at the eucharist be entrusted to mature and respected married men, reserving to celibate priests only the fullness of the ministry, that "holy service of the Gospel" that claims a man totally. That, it is said, would correspond to the deepest meaning of the charismatic office of the presbyterate. Only by looking at the problem in this way will it be possible to resolve it decisively. The way in which the Church approaches the future is something that she must determine for herself.

SELECT BIBLIOGRAPHY

FRANCE

(a) *Books*

P. Hermand, *Condition du Prêtre: Mariage ou Célibat* (Paris, 1963).
P. Winninger, *Pouvoir d'Ordre et Devoir d'Ordre, le Recrutement sacerdotal, le Célibat ecclésiastique* (Strasbourg, 1964).
——— *Mariage et Célibat* (Paris, 1965).
M. Oraison, *Le Célibat. Aspect négatif—réalites positives* (Paris, 1966).

J. Audet, *Mariage et Célibat dans le Service pastoral de l'Eglise: Histoire et Orientation* (Paris, 1967).

M. Bellet, *La Peur ou la Foi. L'Analyse du Prêtre* (Paris, 1967).

T. Matura, *Célibat et Communauté* (Paris, 1967).

J. Pohier, *Psychologie et Théologie* (Paris, 1967).

(b) *Articles*

D. Salman, "De la Fidélité dans de Célibat ecclésiastique et dans le Mariage chrétien," in *Supplément de la Vie Spirituelle* 16 (1963), pp. 257ff.

L. Beirnaert, "Célibat sacerdotal et Sexualité," in *Etudes* (March, 1964), pp. 366ff.

J. Galot, "Sacerdoce et Célibat," in *Nouvelle Revue théologique* (February, 1964), pp. 133ff.

M. Metzger, "Prêtres célibataires et Prêtres mariés," in *Supplément de la Vie Spirituelle* 18 (1965), pp. 208ff.

M. Bellet, "Prêtre pour la Liberté," in *Informations catholiques internationales* 302 (December 15, 1967), pp. 28f.

B. Gardey, "Le Célibat sacerdotal met en Question notre Culture," in *Supplément de la Vie Spirituelle* 21 (1968), pp. 222ff.

M. Oraison, "Le Débat sur le Célibat des Prêtres," in *Le Monde* 9 and 10 (April, 1968).

THE NETHERLANDS

(a) *Books*

Anonymous, *Celibaatscrisis. Suggesties van een priester* (The Hague, 1963).

E. Schillebeeckx, *Het Ambts-Celibaat in de branding* (Bildhoven, 1966).

(b) *Articles*

B. Cardinal Alfrink, "Over het priesterlijk Celibaat," in *Katholiek Archief* 18 (1963), pp. 946ff.

R. Bunnik, "Kerkelijk ambtsdrager en huwelijk," in *Te Elfder Ure* 11 (1964), pp. 249ff.

P. van Belkom, "Opvoeding tot celibaat," in *De Nieuwe Mens* 16 (1964), pp. 25ff.

J. Gronheid, "Het celibaat van de priester, teken van het Godsrijk," in *De Nieuwe Mens* 16 (1964), pp. 19ff.

R. Bunnik, "Het zielzorgelijk tekort. Concilie en Celibaat," in *Te Elfder Ure* 13 (1966), pp. 137ff.

———— "De theologische studie van virginiteit en ambtscelibaat," in *Tijdschrift voor Theologie* 6 (1966), pp. 148ff.

F. Thijssen, "Het Ambts-Celibaat in een open dialoog," in *Theologie en Zielzorg* 62 (1966), pp. 352ff.

GERMANY

(a) *Books*

M. Pfliegler, *Der Zölibat* (Einsiedeln, 1965).

M. Catholicus, *Um den Zölibat* (Zurich, 1966).

———— *Um die Meinungsfreiheit. Das Diskussionsforum um "Zölibat" und "Kirche"* (Nuremberg, 1968).

G. Hamburger, *Katholische Priesterehe oder der Tod eines Tabus?* (Hamburg, 1968).

F. Bockle (ed.), *Der Zölibat* (Mainz, 1968).

L. Rinser, *Zölibat und Frau* (Wurzburg, ^{2} 1968).

T. Kopp, *Zölibat heute. Beiträge zu einem Glaubensgespräch* (Leutesdorf am Rhein, 1968).

A. Antweiler, *Zum Pflichtzölibat der Weltpriester* (Münster, 1968).

B. Kotting, *Der Zölibat in der alten Kirche* (Münster, 1968).

(b) *Articles*

B. Haring *et al.,* "Der Zölibat des Priesters," in *Theologie der Gegenwart* 9 (1966), pp. 125ff.

K. Rahner, "Der Zölibat des Weltpriesters im gegenwärtigen Gespräch," in *Geist und Leben* 40 (1967), pp. 122ff.; 41 (1968), pp. 285ff.

F. Wulf, "Der Christologische Aspekt des priesterlichen Zölibats," in *Seminarium* 19 (1967), pp. 774ff.; reprinted in *Geist und Leben* 41 (1968), pp. 106ff.

———— "Enzyklika über den priesterlichen Zölibat," in *Nachkonziliare Dokumentation* 8 (Trier, 1968), pp. 9-26.

P. Picard, "Die gegenwärtige Diskussion um die priesterliche Existenz," in *Geist und Leben* 41 (1968), pp. 21ff.

E. Klinger, "Der Zölibat von der Ehe her gesehen," in *Geist und Leben* 41 (1968), pp. 377ff.

S. Kraft, "Zur Vereinbarkeit von geistlichem Amt und Ehe," in *Der Seelsorger* 38 (1968), pp. 312ff.

PART III

DOCUMENTATION
CONCILIUM

Office of the Executive Secretary
Nijmegen, Netherlands

Concilium General Secretariat/*Nijmegen, Netherlands*

The Renewal of the Training for the Priesthood

Just as Vatican Council II linked the *Decree on the Ministry and Life of Priests* with the *Decree on Priestly Training,* so it seemed right to incorporate in this volume, which deals with the priest's function and life in the modern world, an article on the renewal of his training. One may wonder whether this is possible, since it has been said several times in this volume that we cannot foresee with certainty what the image of the priest will be like in the future. Yet, in the meantime the reality of the Church's life forces us to continue with the work of training priests, and many publications of recent date show that there is great interest in this renewal.[1]

[1] G. Cenacchi, *La pedagogia seminaristica nei documenti del Magisterio Ecclesiastico* (Rovigo, 1966);, J. Crottogini, *Priester-Presbyter. Beiträge zu einem neuen Priesterbild* (Luzern, 1968); A. Greeley, *The Hesitant Pilgrim* (New York, 1966), esp. Ch. 16; G. Griesl, *Berufung und Lebensform des Priesters* (Innsbruck, 1967); H. E. Hess and H. E. Tödt, *Reform der theologischen Ausbildung. Untersuchungen, Berichte, Empfehlungen* I (Stuttart/Berlin, 1967); J. Lee, *Seminary Education in a Time of Change* (Notre Dame, 1965); G. Martil Barbero, *Los Seminarios en el Concilio Vaticano II. Historia y Comentario* (Salamanca, 1966); J. Potel, J. Maitre and P. Huot-Pleuroux, *Le Clergé français* (Paris, 1967); H. Stenger, *Wissenschaft und Zeugnis. Die Ausbildung des katholischen Seelsorgeklerus in psychologischer Sicht* (Salzburg, 1961); W. D. Wagner, *The Seminary—Protestant and Catholic* (New York, 1966); L. Waltermann, *Klerus zwischen Wissenschaft und Seelsorge. Zur Reform der Priesterausbildung* (Essen, 1966); *Seminary in Crisis* (New York, 1965); *Die Ausbildung der Theologiestudenten in den West-euro-*

The Seminaries: A Precarious Situation

Although the seminaries do not everywhere show the same problems to the same extent, the questions regarding the way of life, the system and content of study, the pastoral formation and openness toward the world may be taken as universally present. They are as much alive in Ceylon as at the Gregorianum or in Latin America. The main factors which made a renewal of training an urgent issue are the decrease in the numbers of candidates for the priesthood, a strong decline in the number of actual priests, the unrest in the seminaries and the fact that the seminary system has fallen into discredit.

While life in the Church became more intense during and because of Vatican Council II, the number of candidates and priests declined considerably each year. Although this tendency could already be observed before the Council,[2] the process seems to have accelerated afterward.[3]

Unrest at the seminaries was occasionally noisy enough to attract the attention of the daily press. In March 1966, seminarians demonstrated in front of the archbishop's residence in Boston. In October of the same year the seminary of Mariana in Brazil was closed for a period of time when it became clear that the majority of the students were against celibacy and against the way in which they were prepared for the priesthood. After some incidents the seminary of San Sebastián in Spain was also closed for several months. During 1968 the seminary of Guarda in Portugal seems to be passing through such a crisis that it is practically empty. Seminarians appear to be dissatisfied with the pat-

---

päischen Ländern (Maastricht, 1965); "Documento final de Medellín, segunda conferencia general del episcopado latinoamericano, XIII, Formación del Clero," in *Criterio* 41, 1558 (Oct. 24, 1968), pp. 794-97.

[2] "De Ontwikkeling van de Priesterroeping in West-Europa," in *Pro Mundi Vita* 4 (1965).

[3] "For the first time all countries of Western Europe are affected by the vocation crisis": *Inf. Cath. Intern.* 287, 12 (1967); for Latin America, see J. Comblin, "Problèmes sacerdotaux d'Amérique Latine," in *La Vie Spir.* 118 (1968), pp. 319-43.

tern of life imposed upon them and also with their education.[4] The problem, too, of the uncertainty about the role and status of the priest [5] seems to exercise a negative influence. Seminarians do not wish to be men that do not belong to the world,[6] and there is more and more evidence that the seminarians want to be qualified in some secular profession. Thus in 1968, 470 Spanish major seminarians interrupted their studies to go out to work or to start qualifying themselves in some secular profession. In both cases the aim was to improve themselves for their priestly function in the future.[7]

Insofar as education is concerned, the seminary is now hardly accepted as an educational institution by the faithful in Western secularized society. Criticism is launched first of all against minor seminaries and then also against major seminaries.[8] Apart from the intellectual formation given there, the psychological and social context in which it is conveyed no longer has appeal. Pierre Reginald Cren, O.P., speaks here of a "social uprooting".[9]

The Decree on Priestly Training (Optatam Totius)

The origin of this Decree [10] shows that the bishops wholly agreed to a new orientation. Instead of the defensive starting points of the decree of the Council of Trent and the powerful

[4] Cf., e.g., Inf. Cath. Intern. 310, 16 (1968). The Spanish episcopal commission for the seminaries signed a declaration which described the tensions prevailing among seminarians. They demanded better formation, particularly in dialogue, better knowledge and closer contact with the world they will have to serve.

[5] M. Oraison, "Un homme sans métier," in Christus 12 (1965), pp. 462-705. According to an investigation by R. Hodge in 1964, the prestige of the priest in America has fallen from the 18th place in a comparative professional table drawn up for the period 1947-1963 to the 21st (mentioned by W. de Bont, in Suppl. de la Vie Spir. 20 (1967), pp. 358-59.

[6] In America people speak of "the hyphenated priest", as a man who lives in the world and is not of the world: W. H. Dodd, "Towards a Theology of Priesthood," in Theol. Studies 28 (1967), pp. 683-705.

[7] Inf. Cath. Intern. 310, 16 (1968).

[8] D. Braun, Priesterroeping en Seminarie (Haarlem, 1964).

[9] "Les Prêtres," in Lum. et Vie 76-77 (1966), pp. 176 and 189.

[10] J. Neuner, "Die Bedeutung und Geschichte des Dekrete über die Ausbildung der Priester," in Das zweite Vatikanische Konzil. Dokumente und Kommentare II (Suppl. Lex. f. Theol. u. Kirche), pp. 310-13; "Die Aussprache über die Priesterausbildung," in Herderkorrespondenz 19

centralizing tendency since the middle of the 19th century which was embodied in Canon Law, they wanted to break through clerical isolation and to introduce some freedom in the application of the renewal. The two main points of our Decree are therefore a *cautious openness* and a certain *decentralization and differentiation.*

The Decree is limited to general directives and orientation in view of the application to the particular situations in the various countries and in order to facilitate the revision of the institutes from time to time. The actual form the seminaries and organization of studies must take is left to the respective episcopal conferences, and the main norm for this will be the local pastoral situation (n. 1).

The formation to be given in a seminary runs on three lines: spiritual, academic and pastoral (Chapters IV, V and VI). Spiritual formation must consist principally in helping the student learn how to live according to the Gospel (n. 8). For the academic formation the Decree stresses that philosophy and theology must be more harmoniously organized, and that the spiritual, academic and pastoral training must be one organic whole (nn. 13-18), and here the quality of the lecturers will be decisive (n. 5). A separate chapter is devoted to pastoral instruction (nn. 19-21), and here the support that can be given by pedagogics, psychology and sociology as well as by periodical practical work is accepted.

The seminary system is seen as necessary for the training of a priest (n. 4). This can be taken to mean that the bishops definitely do not want to go back to the irregular and confused situation that existed before Trent, but it states at the same time their agreement with the institution as it developed in history.[11] In this case renewal can only take place within this framework.

(1964/5), pp. 274-78; see also E. Cenacchi, "Decreto conciliare 'Optatam totius Ecclesiae'," in Palestra del Clero (1966), pp. 608f.

11 P. Picard and E. Emrich, *Priesterbildung in der Diskussion* (Mainz, 1967), pp. 109-10; see also "La renovación de los seminarios según el espíritu del Concilio Vaticano II," in *Seminarios* 12 (1966), pp. 351-93.

The Episcopal Synod of 1967

One of the points dealt with by the first episcopal synod was this training for the priesthood as outlined in the conciliar Decree.[12] The debate was led by Cardinal G. Garrone, former bishop of Toulouse and pro-prefect for the Congregation for Catholic Education. The discussions were limited to two questions: (1) the tasks and competence of the episcopal conferences and their relations with the Congregation for Seminaries and Universities, and (2) the proper preparation of those priests involved in seminary education.

The most important results were: (1) the Congregation of Studies, together with the episcopal conferences, will draft a basic plan for the training of priests in the light of *Optatam totius* as the norm for all other initiatives in this field; (2) every episcopal conference will set up a special commission, consisting of both clergy and laity; (3) the episcopal conferences will set up special institutes or at least special courses for priests who will be involved in seminary training.

It is clear that the organizational process of this renewal demands closer cooperation between the Congregation for Catholic Education and the episcopal conferences, and one hopes that the function of the Congregation here will be rather to serve than to lay down regulations. The questions that are really important— namely, what kind of image of the priest is envisaged, the nature and purpose of the New Testament priesthood and the function of the priest, questions which precede any clear training project —were barely touched upon. There were a few interventions which pointed out that the renewal should not start exclusively from the new mentality of the younger generation but rather from the profound changes that have affected the pastoral function itself.

[12] R. Rouquette, "Le premier synode épiscopal. La réforme des séminaires," in *Etudes* 328 (1968), pp. 107f.; "Die Diskussion über die Seminarreform," in *Herderkorrespondenz* 21 (1967), pp. 581-85; cf. *Civiltà Catt.* 118 (1967), pp. 194-404.

THE RENEWAL OF THE TRADITIONAL TRAINING

At the episcopal synod, P. Arrupe, head of the Jesuits, put forward a remarkable alternative: should the seminaries be adapted to the demands of our time, be less closed societies, etc., while the institution as such would remain intact, or should the whole training be opened up in the sense that the life of the seminarians would be similar to that of priests in pastoral practice? It is clear that the latter possibility was not envisaged by the Decree of Vatican Council II. The only thought there was that of renewing the traditional training. Nor did it give a clear statement about the alternative of either a general priestly formation, which has at present led to unsatisfactory results in many places,[13] or a definite professional training of priests as such. The renewal does not touch the essential nature of the existing seminary system and is limited to adapting it to the demands of our time.

In this case the renewal can then relate to one of the three lines of the candidate's formation—academic, pastoral and spiritual—which will again exercise a mutual influence on each other.

Academic Training (Scientific-Theological) [14]

A first point to be discussed is the nature of the philosophical and theological training. The adverse criticism of the methods

13 Cf. P. Picard, *op. cit.,* p. 86.

14 *Neuordnung der Theologische Studiën für Priesterkandidaten,* report commissioned by the German hierarchy (1967), and meant to serve as experiment for the next five years; *Rapport over Theologische opleiding in verband met kerkelijk ambtswerk,* commissioned by the Dutch hierarchy (1968), also called the "Report of the Schoonenberg Commission"; "Le premier cycle du grand séminaire," in *Interséminaires* 9 (March 1967), pp. 13-24; A. Antweiler, "Ziel und Spielraum der Priesterausbildung," in *Theol. u. Glaube* 57 (1967), pp. 411-26; 58 (1968), pp. 131-48; M. Longard, W. Göddeke and E. Drewermann, "Rückblick auf das Theologiestudium aus der Perspektive eines Seminaristen," in *Theol.*

used in the classic philosophical and theological textbooks is well known. K. Rahner has pointed out that the Latin method, which provided material that was clearly set out and easy to learn by heart, gave the impression that there were no problems and the debate was closed. At the German universities theology wants to be scientific and professional, but in that case one should re- member the need to begin with offering clear and viable con- cepts. It is the students who point to the situation in which they now find themselves, since theology has abandoned the specula- tive synthesis in favor of analytical and historical-critical inves- tigations. Where the necessary knowledge is lacking for a critical position with regard to partial studies, the result will be frag- mentary knowledge.

It is apparent therefore that the answer does not lie in a real scientific training. This is often unattainable or does not corre- spond to the aim of the training. There is thus a widespread demand for a training that is more pastorally oriented.[15] But one can examine the nature of a scientific training. On this point the discussion is well advanced in Holland. The report of the Schoonenberg commission shows that, apart from theological training in the framework of academic (university) education, there is room for a theological training in the framework of higher professional education which must be understood as a practically oriented education, not leading to academic qualifica- tion, but giving the students scientifically responsible training in practical abilities, methods and techniques of communication, and so on.[16]

---

u. *Glaube* 56 (1966), pp. 48-53; K. Rahner, "Zur Neuordnung der Theologische Studien," in *St. der Zeit* 93 (1968), pp. 1-22; F. Tollu, "Le renouveau des Grands Séminaires. Regard sur le travail en cours," in *Suppl. de la Vie Spir.* 20 (1967), pp. 22-40; *idem*, "Recherches sur le programme des études dans les grands séminaires," in *Interséminaires* 13 (March 1968), pp. 29-36; H. Zimmerman, "Reform des Theologiestu- diums aus der Sicht des Professors," in *Theol. u. Glaube* 56 (1966), pp. 24-35; "Le Renouveau des Grands Séminaires," in *Etudes* 327 (1967), pp. 93-107.

[15] Cf., e.g., A. Antweiler, *art. cit.*, p. 138.
[16] Report of the Schoonenberg Commission, n. 4.

For full-time pastors, however, the report only sees value in academic theological training at university level. In that case the point is not practical ability in scientific techniques but a critical and scientific way of thinking and working. But there must be theological formation because the religious context of the pastor's functions makes it clear that only the study of theology is the proper professional training for the priest's office.[17] For those who have received their theological formation in the framework of higher professional education (assistants or workers with a specialized function) [18] the report foresees the desirability and possibility of an ordination to priesthood or diaconate or no ordination at all, according to their task and the milieu in which they operate. In this the Dutch commission has only partially met the problems connected with other possible ways of training for the priestly office apart from the academic theological training at the university level.

Even when starting from a theological training at the university level, there remains the question of practical, existential principles for building up a study project based on the aim of theological training. From this point of view Rahner sees the new German study plan as "maintaining what already exists", a new timetable for existing subjects.[19] The plan rightly says that the guiding principle must be a training based on the later functional and priestly occupation,[20] but this is understood so generally that nothing has come of it. Here we may expect something more from the training program for the major seminaries in France, the main lines of which were laid down at the plenary gather-

---

[17] *Ibid.*, n. 3.
[18] By this the report means full-time or part-time experts in practical work in a comprehensive pastoral setup—among other things for religious instruction, pastoral-clinical guidance, ecclesiastical development work, training and group work, and parochial assistants for liturgy and catechetics.
[19] K. Rahner (*art. cit.*, p. 13) says: "The aim of the basic training is not to produce a young specialist but rather a Christian and priest in his own personal existence today, and the ordinary pastor, who can hold their own also with a modern educated person."
[20] *Neuordnung* (n. 14), A, 1.

ings of the French hierarchy in the autumn of 1966 and 1967.[21] The whole training will be based on a threefold division: a first cycle of two years in which the mystery of salvation, among other things, must become a living reality for the young students [22] and be linked with an introductory philosophy centered on "man"; [23] then a period during which the students pass through various phases, distinguished as "probationary stages" and "stages for training in the apostolate"; and, finally, a second cycle where, for the most part, study is pastorally oriented. It is noteworthy that, in contrast to the German plan, no attempt is made to give this training a university structure, and that it is less likely to become a practical higher professional education as some want it to be in Holland. It is rather a spiritual education, seen as an initiation and as having a powerful missionary and apostolic tendency.

Pastoral Training [24]

The *Decree on Priestly Training* had previously emphasized the importance and necessity of pastoral formation. What is new here is the emphasis on the importance of practical exercises in various forms of the apostolate and the need to learn to work as a team. These are essential important elements of pastoral training, and the entire concept entails a fundamental change in the traditional view of seminary training. We may thus reach a new concept of the "seminary" as something in terms of a definite

[21] Cf. *Herderkorresp.* 22 (1968), pp. 400-01.

[22] "First demand: that theology is done from the beginning in the shape of some overall and systematic support to the training, centered on the mystery of salvation through Christ": *Intersém.* 9, p. 14.

[23] "Second demand: that this cycle include basic moral teaching and some philosophy in depth to provide a serious understanding of man, his conscience, his situation in the world and in relation to God, the universe, society and history" (*ibid.*).

[24] *Decree on Priestly Training,* nn. 19-21; "Guide pastoral pour les stages longs des grands séminaristes," in *Intersémin.* 13 (March 1968), pp. 21-28; "Cursus Pastorale Vorming voor binnen en buitenland," in *Studiegids 1968-9. Stichting Theologische Faculteit te Tilburg,* pp. 57-62; E. Marcus, "L'initiation au ministère," in J. Frisque *et al., Les Prêtres* (Paris, 1968), pp. 345-71; B. Frison, "Training in the Seminary," in *The Jurist* 27 (1967), pp. 323-49.

time rather than in terms of a definite place.[25] The period of the various stages is not yet conceived as time spent outside the seminary.

Pastoral training will consist in theoretical explanations and putting into practice the new opportunity of becoming familiar beforehand with pastoral work during the study years by engaging in such activity under supervision. It will be a difficult task to integrate both these requirements into the whole plan of theological training. Thus the provisional German plan foresees two semesters of pastoral training in (or based on) the seminary after ten semesters of university study. The pastoral course is meant to be the practical introduction to pastoral care, but at the same time it must serve to deepen the spiritual and ascetical aspect of priestly training.[26]

It has been rightly pointed out that this procedure pulls the scientific and the priestly training completely apart.[27] The aim of pastoral formation is to actively direct theological training to pastoral situations. This requires "the fostering of a basic attitude which enables one to see the whole concrete reality of life in the light of the faith and to approach it constructively, aware of one's talents and limitations, and of the need for cooperation and communication with others".[28] The French idea about pastoral stages is more or less the same, although it stresses the ecclesial dimension more explicitly. In such a stage the "probationer" must be able to see the life of the Church in her missionary effort, with successes and failures in the most varied tasks. These stages will undoubtedly be emphasized at the end of the training to ensure their greatest effectiveness, but they must be integrated in the whole.

In France the stages are typically defined as an "experimental

---

[25] Cf., for instance, the project for the setting up of an "Institut de formation d'éducateurs du Clergé," approved by the French hierarchy at Lourdes, Nov. 1967. Cf. *Intersém.* 13, p. 12.

[26] *Neuordnung* (cf. n. 14), B, I, 1.

[27] "Scheitert die Reform des Theologiestudiums?" in *Herderkorresp.* 22 (1968), pp. 105-08, esp. p. 106.

[28] Cf. *Studiegids Tilburg*, p. 57; cf. "Guide pastorale," in *Intersém.* 13, p. 27.

initiation into the office", or as initiation into the presbyterium, a process which implies both incorporation and mission.[29] In concrete terms it means that the Church must incorporate her priests in the pastoral love which is embodied in the presbyterium, and in the relations with the faithful and the non-believers. This requires of those responsible for pastoral training that they give their function a concrete ecclesial dimension.

These pastoral stages will undoubtedly be developed in very different ways. It has been suggested that studies should be interrupted for at least one year. Others demand that this pastoral training should be absorbed in the actual time devoted to study by breaking it up into many short periods, on the grounds that this would be more profitable from the point of view of discussion and reflection.[30] In any event, that such pastoral training will be put into practice everywhere in one way or another seems a foregone conclusion.[31]

Spiritual Formation

The unrest in the seminaries and among priests seems to be largely due to the way of life imposed upon them, and not essentially to the idea of the priesthood as such.[32] In order to become a priest the candidate must conform to a large amount of definite social and religious traditions, customs and rules. Noteworthy here are the conclusions reached in a recent investigation of the usual norms by which a candidate is judged fit for the priestly office in a Dutch seminary.[33] It appeared that the less intelligent, the more conservative, and the more rigidly religious candidates had a better chance of being accepted. The aim of the seminary

[29] E. Marcus, *art. cit.,* pp. 348f.

[30] K. Nichols, "Education and the Formation of Priests," in *Clergy Review* 52 (1967), pp. 294-99.

[31] *Inf. Cath. Int.* has reported on the Seminary of Trent (Italy) and that of John XXIII (Louvain, Belgium) in n. 279, 19 (1967), on Spain in n. 310, 16 (1968); for East Africa, cf. *Clergy Review* 53 (1968), pp. 170-71.

[32] *Inf. Cath. Int.* 311, 23 (1968).

[33] W. J. Berger, *Beoordeling van geschiktheid voor het priesterambt* (Nijmegen, 1968).

system as it developed since Trent was precisely the fostering of a particularly "sacerdotal" style of life and the formation of a priestly character that would fit into every priestly situation.[34]

Spiritual formation is a complex whole. In fact, it embraces both religious formation and the formation of the personality.[35] In the matter of guiding the students, the two aspects must therefore at least be distinguished, however closely they are connected. One might speak here of a guidance of "psychological welfare" and "pastoral guidance".[36] Both these aspects can be found in the *Decree on Priestly Training*. This attaches great importance to leading the candidate to adulthood. Candidates should be accepted only when they have reached human and Christian adulthood (n. 6). The norms of a Christian education must be respected, taken into consideration and supplemented with the most recent findings of sound psychology and pedagogics (n. 11). How these general and not yet meaningful principles must be critically applied to training for the priesthood only becomes clear when "the most recent findings of sound psychology and pedagogics" are put into practice.[37] Here the importance of work (study and the exercise of the priestly function, but also secular work) for the self-realization of man, the importance of

[34] Cf. J. Rogé, *Le simple Prêtre* (Paris, 1965), esp. pp. 79-154.

[35] The Schoonenberg Report speaks of a "personal formation and a religious formation" (n. 2). In the same way C. Fielding, in his *Education for Ministry* (Dayton, 1966), mentions "four goals of professional theological education" (p. 50): "1. the acquisition of knowledge (theological training); 2. the development of professional skill (pastoral training); 3 and 4. personal (human) growth and deepening of Christian commitment (spiritual formation)." He points out that we seem to have no proper terms for the last two. "Emotional maturity" he considers too limited, and words such as "piety", "spirituality" or "religious devotion" hardly convey the full meaning of "Christian discipleship".

[36] Cf. "Pastorale beleidslijnen voor de ambtsvervulling van de priester in Nederland," in *Pastorale Gids* (Publ. by the Pastoral Inst. of the Dutch Province).

[37] A. Vergote, "Réflexions psychologiques sur le devenir humain et chrétien du prêtre," in *Le Prêtre et le monde sécularisé* (Report on the Luzern Congress of Sept. 1967, in a special issue of the *Bulletin d'inform. de l'Inst. pour l'Entraide Sacerdotale en Europe* (Maastricht, 1968), pp. 63-82).

an integrated sexuality (celibacy) and the concrete implications
of all this become clear.

Of course, the Decree also deals extensively with religious
training (nn. 8-12). Here Christ and his Church are put in the
center, and the ideal could be summarized as a spirituality of the
imitation of Christ and of disinterested service.[38] Remarkably
little is said about the practice of "spiritual exercises" (n. 8).
However, the episcopal synod showed how much importance was
attached to this. There was still a clinging to a special priestly
spirituality, and this expressed itself in complaints about the ne-
glect of pious exercises and the loss of sound spirituality. On this
point there is more realism and more hope in the way A. Vergote
described the modern situation.[39] Students for the priesthood
appear to be suffering particularly from emotional immaturity—
hence their uncertainty and, for instance, their almost bodily fear
of becoming alienated from the world. One should not ask too
much of these young people. Vergote insists that religious training should be a very gradual process, so that there is a genuine
chance of integrating the human and Christian dimensions as the
foundation of a true attitude of faith.[40] On the other hand, the
importance of spiritual training should not be underrated. Religion and religious attitudes are not created merely by reflection
(theology) and experience (pastoral work). The spiritual
"hunch", hope and faith play an important part here. One can
"learn" the facts and interpretations of religion, but not religion
as a "conviction" and an encounter with God.[41]

The keynote of this whole renewal movement seems to be the
attempt to strike a balance between theoretical theological training and the practical pastoral training. Many efforts are being
made to renew the training and to make seminary life possible in

[38] P. Picard, "Hinführung der zukünftigen Priester zum Knechtdienst
Christi," in Geist u. Leben 40 (1967), pp. 360-80.
[39] Cf. above, n. 37.
[40] Cf. C. Dumont, "Pour une conversion 'anthropocentrique' dans la
formation des clercs," in Nouv. Rev. Théol. 97 (1965), pp. 449-65.
[41] Cf. A. Antweiler, in Theol. u. Glaube 58 (1968), pp. 147-48.

the spirit of Vatican Council II. Two rather recent developments must still be mentioned here, the concentration of several seminaries into one and the formation of *équipes* for the purpose of living or working together within a seminary. In Holland the education provided by almost all of the 48 seminaries has been concentrated in five higher educational institutes for theology and the existing school of theology at the University of Nijmegen which is now being enlarged for this purpose.[42] Something similar is happening in Belgium although the concentration is so far limited to the regular clergy.[43] In Spain the six dioceses of the province of Granada have decided to send their seminarians to the school of theology at Granada, which will now function as a regional seminary.[44] France has its own way of doing this in what is called a "consortium" (literally, a group of enterprises working together for a common purpose). This is connected with the new seminary training in France which proceeds, as pointed out above, in two cycles. Thus the Région du Nord provides the first cycle of the training for all at Soissons, and the second cycle at Rheims, and seven dioceses are participating in this.[45]

While this kind of concentration was partly due to the decline in the number of students, it also has the advantage that it makes it possible to provide teams of specialist professors. The emergence of vaster training centers prompted the formation of so-called *équipes,* smaller units in which students live or work together, usually with one of the priests of the seminary. This has happened particularly in France, but also, for instance, in the Seminary of John XXIII at Louvain. It is, on the one hand, an attempt to make the environment more livable, and, on the other,

[42] See the sections on the renewal of priestly training in Holland under the heading "Seminarie" in *Pastorale Gids.*

[43] The most important concentration will probably be the "Centrum voor kerkelijke Studies" of Louvain.

[44] *Inf. Cath. Intern.* 290, 10 (1967).

[45] "Situation des grands séminaires de France," in *Intersémin.* 13 (March 1968) and "Vernieuwing van de groot-seminaries in Frankrijk," in *Pastorale Gids,* under the heading "Seminarie".

a training for living and working together in preparation for the comprehensive pastoral work in presbyterium.

SOME FEATURES OF TRAINING
FOR THE PRIESTHOOD IN THE FUTURE

It is to be expected that the present renewal will ultimately bring about a more realistic scientific education, a more solid formation of the personality and a better preparation for pastoral work. But when one looks for solutions to such problems as, for instance, a genuine pluralization or professionalization of the priestly office, or the real professional function of the pastor, or the profound changes affecting the relation between the Church and the world, then we see that this kind of adaptation does not give us the structure of the future. At present, however, we are not yet prepared to let go of the past. Even the "open" seminary still aims at the formation of the young clergy by requiring them to live together in an all-embracing community.[46] We can see a first attempt at breaking through this wall in the process of de-clericalization.[47]

A Secularized Training

One of the results of the process of secularization is that the categories of "sacred" and "profane" are no longer considered absolute but relative.[48] And so it becomes difficult to still speak of a specific sacerdotal way of life, a sacerdotal spirituality, etc. His vocation is the same as that of every Christian, whatever his state of life or profession. The project of a man's life is either

[46] "Community of Study, Community of Worship, Community of Life," in J. Keller and R. Armstrong, *Apostolic Renewal in the Seminary in the Light of Vatican II* (New York, 1965), p. 13.

[47] J. Duquesne, "Il faut 'déclérifier' le sacerdoce," in *Inf. Cath. Int.* 311 (1968), pp. 23-24; I. Illich, "The Vanishing Clergyman," in *The Critic* (1967); cf. H. C. Laan, *De rooms-katholieke Kerkorganisatie in Nederland* (Utrecht, 1967), pp. 208-11.

[48] Cf. M.-D. Chenu's article in this volume.

Christian or un-Christian.[49] From this point of view it is then difficult to think of a special training for the priesthood which must lead to a state of life and which is seen as the necessary condition for exercising the ecclesiastical office. The distinction of functions does not require an ontological substratum to serve as the basis for this distinction.[50]

The phenomenon of secularization also leads to the disappearance of the ghetto church or the so-called "people's church" (*Volkskirche*). Although this will not necessarily lead to the disappearance of the "institutional" Church, the "image" is bound to be profoundly affected.[51] As an institution the Church will be less tied up with the structures of society, but, on the other hand, she will be much more closely united to the ordinary life of human beings. Ecclesiastical training, which will probably be of short duration, whether professional or not, will take place not in isolation, but right in the middle of ordinary life. Significant here is that in Holland this training now takes place in those five higher institutes of theology in urban centers instead of the old fifty different institutes for philosophy and theology that were spread out over the countryside. Now it is possible to develop a training which is in contact with the urbanized culture of the country. The same situation (though in a very different perspective) must be able to develop in countries where a non-Western culture prevails. There, too, we must be able to develop a training which does not alienate the trainees from their own people which is not divorced from the national culture.[52] The fact remains, of course, that the priestly—or, rather, the Christian—mission will always include elements of renunciation

---

[49] L. A. H. Smits, "Werkelijkheidszin in de opleiding tot kerkelijke dienst," in G. C. Anawati *et al., Missionaire Wegen voor Morgen* (Hilversum and Brussels, 1967).

[50] F. Haarsma, "Einige Pastoral-theologischen Thesen über den Priester," in *Der Priester in einer säkularisierten Welt*, pp. 107-14.

[51] Cf., e.g., "Als 'freischwebende' spezialistische Institution für die Sinnfragen," in O. Schreuder, *ibid.,* p. 85.

[52] M. Mihayo, "African Clergy," in *Clergy Review* 53 (1968), pp. 170-77. Cf. *Herderkorrespondenz* 19 (1964-5), p. 244.

in the sense of prophetic witness within one's own environment. As a true proclaimer of salvation one cannot surrender to one's culture or environment.[53]

Pluriformity or Differentiation

Uniformity of training, as envisaged by the Tridentine decree, will disappear. Vatican Council II has already created the possibility of some differentiation in the various countries.[54] But the Council nowhere touched upon the necessity of establishing a whole gamut of possibilities within the actual training system. It still remains to be seen how far the differences in training that will arise in various countries will be able to break through the uniformity which beset the priestly office before the Council. In the meantime a plea has been made in several quarters for a genuine differentiation of the office, based on the needs of the ecclesial communities and the officeholders themselves. The report of the Schoonenberg Commission rightly stated that these needs must be tested by reference to the Gospel. But it is a fact that the need to provide every opportunity for this pluriformity to develop [55] is bound to lead to pluriformity in training and a differentiation which goes further than is as yet possible, and this will come about through a sharper definition of the various functions which all belong to the service of the ministry.

This requires a clear distinction of the various functions so that an adequate training can be laid down or developed. The functions of the Church as a whole allow us to distinguish the following four: preaching, liturgy, community guidance and pastoral work.[56] Translated into terms of personal functions, this gives us a scale which runs from prophet, preacher, theologian, catechist and the leader of the liturgical service down to the pastor—precisely that whole mixture which is today expected of

[53] P. Picard, op. cit., p. 364.

[54] Even the Tridentine decree left the bishops more freedom than they used. See P. Declerck, "Het seminariedecreet van Trente," in Coll. Brug. et Gand. 11 (1965), pp. 1-36.

[55] See the 9th resolution of the Luzern Congress; also cf. n. 37 above.

[56] See E. Pin's article in this volume, and F. Haarsma, art. cit. in n. 50, p. 112.

every priest. Now it is clearly possible to train somebody as a theologian, a catechist or one who is equipped with specific pastoral techniques, but it is more difficult to train a preacher and practically impossible to train a prophet, because there is nothing to guarantee the enduring character of the charism of prophecy. Nor does it seem suitable to give adolescents a direct training in community guiding, since this demands that one is called to it on the basis of qualities which have already become manifest.[57]

Professionalization

By this term we mean a professional training which makes someone competent to discharge a specific function. Here F. Haarsma distinguishes two possibilities in connection with the priestly office: the functionary with a clearly defined function and competence in society, and the prophet who wants the message to be understood where it has not yet been listened to.[58] Where the intention is to train adolescents for the priestly office, this is only meaningful in our present situation, in the framework of Western society, as a professional training.[59] In spite of all the objections to any consideration of a professionalization of the priestly office (the nature of the priesthood cannot be wholly contained in its functions), the choice between a training of amateur theologians and a clear professional training is not difficult. On the one hand, the young priests' uncertainty about their function is sufficiently significant, and, on the other, it is difficult to see how the office can keep functioning in the Church in this secularized pluriform society which demands professional tech-

[57] J. Kerkhofs, "De priester in een geseculariseerde wereld," in *Streven* 21 (1967-8), pp. 172-78.
[58] "Die wiederherstellung des Profetischen im Priester," in *Der Seelsorger* 36 (1966), pp. 392-97.
[59] This does not mean that these people are called exclusively to the priestly service. O. Schreuder foresees the following possible distinctions: men who exercise an ecclesiastical function as a profession and an office (e.g., bishop, pastor), others who belong professionally but do not have the office (professional theologians, catechists), and those who have an office but do not exercise it professionally (part-time priests). He sees the vocation of the layman neither as professional nor as implying an office. Cf. *supra*, n. 51.

niques for our proclamation. O. Schreuder has given some illustrations of this point. Instead of methods of indoctrination, we must have a genuine proclamation of the faith which presupposes a knowledge of the insights provided by the science of mass-communication. Instead of ritualism we must have a liturgy that can play with the expressive nature of word and symbols, and this presupposes a knowledge of the techniques of social psychology. Instead of social control we must have individual group proclamation and pastoral consultation, and this again presupposes a knowledge of the techniques of dialogue and pastoral counseling.

All of this may perhaps be summarized as follows. Much of what is taking place in the field of renewal today still falls in the perspective of a renewal of the traditional training. Here professionalization and differentiation have a part to play, but these two factors operate inevitably in favor of totally new structures.

BIOGRAPHICAL NOTES

KARL SCHELKLE: Born in Germany in 1908, he was ordained in 1932. He studied at the universities of Tübingen and Bonn, receiving doctorates in philosophy and theology. He is professor of New Testament theology at the Catholic Theological Faculty of Tübingen University. His publications include the three-volume work *Jungerschaft und Apostelamt* (1965) and *Priester und Laien in der Kirche* (1968).

WALTER KASPER: Born in Germany in 1933, he was ordained in 1957. He studied at the universities of Tübingen and Munich, receiving a doctorate in theology. He is professor of dogmatic theology at the University of Münster. His publications include *Das Absolute in der Geschichte, Philosophie und Theologie der Geschichte in der Spätphilosophie Schellings* (Mainz, 1965) and *Dogma unter dem Wort Gottes* (Mainz, 1967).

ADRIAN HASTINGS: Born in Malaya in 1929, he was ordained in 1955. He studied in England at the universities of Oxford and Cambridge, and in Rome, receiving a doctorate in theology. He is currently editor of the bi-monthly bulletin *Post-Vatican II* for the clergy of East Africa, and he is on the editorial board of *The African Ecclesiastical Review*. His published works include *Church and Mission in Modern Africa* (Burns & Oates, 1967).

EMILE PIN, S.J.: Born in France in 1921, he was ordained in 1953. He studied in France at the universities of Grenoble, Montpellier, Paris and Lyons, and in America at the University of Chicago. He earned licentiates in law and theology and a doctorate in sociology. At present he is professor of sociology and director of the Centre of Social Research at the Gregorian in Rome. His published works include *Les Classes sociales* (Paris, 1962) and (jointly with F. Houtart) *L'Église à l'heure de l'Amérique Latine* (Paris, 1965).

FRANS HAARSMA: Born in Holland in 1921, he was ordained in 1947. He studied at the Catholic University of Nijmegen, receiving a doctorate in theology. He is now professor of pastoral theology at Nijmegen. His publications include *Geest en Kerk. Een pastoraal-oecumenische studie over de ecclesiologie van Dr O. Noordmans* (Utrecht, 1967).

195

HEINZ SCHUSTER: Born in Germany in 1930, he was ordained in 1955. He studied at the University of Innsbruck, and in Germany at the Theological Faculty of Trier, receiving a doctorate in theology. He is professor of theology and of catechetics at the Catechetical High School at Saarbrücken in Germany. He is the author of "Geschichte der Pastoraltheologie; Wesen und Aufgabe der Pastoral Theologie" in Volume I of *Handbuch der Pastoraltheologie* (Freiburg, 1964), and, jointly with N. Greinacher, "Elite und Masse" in Volume II (Freiburg, 1965).

KARL RAHNER, S.J.: Born in Germany in 1904, he was ordained in 1932. He studied at the universities of Freiburg im Breisgau and Innsbruck. He holds a doctorate in theology, and is professor of dogma and the history of dogma at the University of Münster. His many important publications include the eight-volume *Schriften zur Theologie* (Einsiedeln), *Mission and Grace* (London & New York), and *Servants of the Lord* (London & New York). He is also the editor of the ten-volume work *Lexikon für Theologie und Kirche* (Freiburg im Breisgau).

STEFAN BARELA: Born in Poland in 1916, he was ordained in 1944 and consecrated bishop in 1961. He studied at the University of Jagellon in Cracow, and at the Catholic University of Lublin. He gained his doctorate in 1950, and is currently bishop of Czestochowa. He is the author of several articles on the spirituality of the priesthood.

NORBERT GREINACHER: Born in Freiburg im Breisgau in 1931, he was ordained in 1956. He studied at the universities of Freiburg im Breisgau, Vienna and Paris, gaining his doctorate in theology. He is dean of studies at the University of Münster. His published works include *Die Kirche in der städtische Gesellschaft* (Mainz, 1966).

AUGUSTIN ANDREU-RODRIGO: Born in Spain in 1928, he was ordained in 1953. He studied at the Oriental Institute in Rome, and in 1963 obtained his doctorate in Eastern Church studies. He is professor of dogma at the Major Seminary of Valencia, Spain. He has published an important article on marriage ("Matrimonio") in the *Enciclopedia de la Biblia* (Barcelona) and two contributions to *Apostolado Sacerdotal* (1966) on the liturgy in priestly life and on the theological content of the *Constitution on the Church*.

MARIE-DOMINIQUE CHENU, O.P.: Born in Paris in 1895, he was ordained in 1918. He studied at the Angelicum in Rome, and gained his doctorate in theology. He has lectured on the history of theology at the Saulchoir and taught at the Sorbonne. His many important works include *Pour une théologie de travail* (Paris, 1955) and *Peuple de Dieu dans le monde* (Paris, 1966).

ILDEFONSO ALVAREZ BOLADO, S.J.: Born in Valladolid in 1928, he was ordained in 1958. He studied in Spain at the University of Barcelona and at the Jesuit Theological Faculty at San Cugat del Vallés, and in Austria at the Theological Faculty of Innsbruck. He holds licentiates in literature and theology and a doctorate in philosophy. He is director of the Institute Fe y Secularidad in Madrid, and is adviser to the papal Secretariat for Non-Believers. His publications include "La Teología Americana de la 'muerte de Dios'," in *Dios-Ateismo* (Deusto, 1968).

JAMES O'CONNELL, S.M.A.: Born in Ireland in 1925, he was ordained in 1952. He studied at the National University of Ireland, and at Louvain. He holds a doctorate in philosophy, and is professor of political science at the University of Ibadan, Nigeria. He is co-author, with L. G. Cowan and D. Scanlon, of *Education and Nation-Building in Africa* (New York, 1965).

ROBERT FOX: Born in New York in 1930, he was ordained in 1955. He studied in America at St. Joseph's Seminary and at the Catholic University of America in Washington. He has a degree in sociology, and is adviser to the Spanish community in New York.

MARIO CUMINETTI: Born in Italy in 1934, he was ordained in 1957. He studied at the Seminary of Bergamo and at the Gregorian, Rome. He gained his doctorate in theology in 1963, and is on the editorial board of *Servizio della Parola*.

THOMAS PUCELIK: Born in America in 1932, he is a priest. He studied in America at St. Thomas College and St. Paul's Seminary, and in Rome at the Angelicum, gaining his doctorate in theology. He is assistant professor of religion at Bradley University in America.

MANUEL EDWARDS, SS.CC.: Born in Santiago in 1914, he was ordained in 1937. He studied at the House of Studies of his Order. He is president of the Confederation of Latin-American Religious.

DANIEL PASU-PASU, S.J.: Born in the Congo in 1921, he was ordained in 1949. He studied in the Congo at the Major Seminary of Mayidi, in Belgium at the Jesuit House of Studies at Eegenhoven, and at the Gregorian in Rome. He holds licentiates in philosophy, theology and sociology. He is professor of economics and sociology at the Jesuit Scholasticate, of Kimuenze, Congo, and editor of the journal *Cadicec*.

ENDA MCDONAGH: Born in Ireland in 1930, he was ordained in 1955. He studied at St. Patrick's College, Maynooth, the Angelicum and Gregorian in Rome, the University of Munich, and the Catholic Institute of Paris. He received doctorates in theology and Canon Law, and is professor of moral theology and Canon Law at St. Patrick's College, Maynooth.

FRIEDRICH WULF, S.J.: Born in Düsseldorf in 1908, he was ordained in 1938. He studied in Germany at the universities of Münster and Tübingen, receiving a doctorate in philosophy. His publications include *Geistliches Leben in der heutigen Welt* (Freiburg, 1960), and he is editor-in-chief of the review *Geist und Leben*.

International Publishers of CONCILIUM

ENGLISH EDITION
Paulist Press
Glen Rock, N.J., U.S.A.

Burns & Oates Ltd.
25 Ashley Place
London, S.W.1

DUTCH EDITION
Uitgeverij Paul Brand, N.V.
Hilversum, Netherlands

FRENCH EDITION
Maison Mame
Tours/Paris, France

JAPANESE EDITION (PARTIAL)
Nansôsha
Tokyo, Japan

GERMAN EDITION
Verlagsanstalt Benziger & Co., A.G.
Einsiedeln, Switzerland

Matthias Grunewald-Verlag
Mainz, W. Germany

SPANISH EDITION
Ediciones Guadarrama
Madrid, Spain

PORTUGUESE EDITION
Livraria Morais Editora, Ltda.
Lisbon, Portugal

ITALIAN EDITION
Editrice Queriniana
Brescia, Italy

POLISH EDITION (PARTIAL)
Pallottinum
Poznan-Warsaw, Poland